# Vaiti of the

Beatrice Grimshaw

## Alpha Editions

This edition published in 2024

ISBN : 9789362097620

Design and Setting By
**Alpha Editions**
www.alphaedis.com
Email - info@alphaedis.com

# Contents

# PROLOGUE

It was in the seventies, long ago.

*     *     *     *     *

Summer—yet a slow grey dawn, lingering long in the sky. August—yet a chilly morning, crisping the landlocked waters of the bay with cold knife-edges of foam. Out at sea, the wild white horses plunging madly under the whip of the sunrise wind; the bar beginning to thunder. Inshore, beneath the green slope of the castle hill, small angry ripples beating and fretting the untrampled sand. Dead rose-leaves from the gardens floating among the seaweed; a torn bird's-nest, flung down by the wind, lying on the edge of the steep cliff pathway.... It was still the time of summer, yet, too surely, autumn had come.

The sodden leaves lay thick in the bottom of the boat when the man seized it by the gunwale and ran it down the beach into the snatching waves.... Oh, an autumn day indeed, here in wild Caithness, though summer was still at its fairest in kinder lands. And in the heart of the man who was rowing fast through the angry dawn light, to the tall schooner yacht that swung and tore at her moorings out in the bay, there was autumn too, with winter close at hand.

All so long ago! who remembers?

Not the newspapers which, in a day or two after, shrieked the scandal broadcast, east and west. Not the guests of the castle house-party—they are dead, or old, which is half of death, since then. Not the Prince whose dignity had been insulted by the outbreak of a vulgar card scandal in his very presence—he struck the titled owner of the house off the list of his intimates forthwith, and then forgot about it and him. Not the colonel of the famous regiment, who found out defalcations in the funds belonging to the mess, a few days after, and knew why his most promising young officer had done the unforgiveable thing—for the Ashanti spears ended life and memory for him out on the African plains, before even Piccadilly had made an end of talking. Not the Royal Yacht Squadron—the reported loss of the famous *Paquita* at sea, with her disgraced owner on board, is a tale that even the oldest *habitue* of Cowes could not tell you to-day.... No one remembers. When the beautiful white schooner spread her wings below the castle wall, and beat her way like a frightened butterfly out to the stormy sea, she sailed away in silence, and she and hers were known no more.

Yet, but for that stormy day in the Highlands, and the boat that fled to sea, these tales of far-off lands had never been told.

# CHAPTER I

## THE PEARL LAGOON

"Where's the old man?"

"Old man drunk," replied Vaiti indifferently. She had learned to play "The Maiden's Prayer," maltreat three European languages, and cultivate a waist in her Tahitian convent school. But that was five years ago now, and Vaiti's "papalangi" verbs had dropped from her quite as soon, and as naturally, as her "Belitani" stays.

"Why can't he wake up and give us an observation?" commented the mate indignantly. "It would be hard if a man mightn't enjoy himself in port; but we're four days out now, and he's as bad as ever, lyin' all the time on the settee like a——"

"You better mind too much what you say my father!" Vaiti had set one shapely olive hand on the deck, and sprung to her feet like a flying-fish making a leap. She was taller than the sturdy, red-haired mate, as she stood up on the poop, her bare feet well apart, her white muslin loose gown swelling out as she leaned to the roll of the steamer, and her black-brown eyes, deep-set under fine brows as straight as a ruler, staring down the blue eyes of the man.

"Very sorry, I'm sure; no offence meant," said the mate humbly. "But we want an observation, and he ain't no good. Why, you know as well as me that he'll be like this, off and on, all the voyage now; we've both of us seen it before."

Vaiti stamped her bare feet on the deck.

"I know—I know! I try all the way from Apia wake him up—no good! I tell you, Alliti"—the mate's name, Harris, usually took this form in the pigeon-English of Polynesia—"this very bad time for him to get 'quiffy. Too much bad time. Never mind. Get the sextan'. I take sun myself."

The mate ran down the companion and into the cabin, where the captain's six feet two of drunken ineptitude sprawled over most of the space available for passing. He stopped for a moment to look at the heavy, unconscious face—a handsome face, with the remains of refinement about it; for Captain Saxon had been a gentleman once, and his name (which was certainly not Saxon then) had appeared among the lists of "members deceased" in the annual reports of all the best London clubs of the 'seventies.... Why Saxon died, and why he came to life again in the South Pacific some years later, is a tale that need not be told, even if it is guessed. Many such substantial ghosts roam the South Seas unexorcised—many a man whose name adorns a memorial tablet, guarded by weeping marble angels, on the walls of some ivied English Church, is busy conferring a peculiar fitness upon the occupation of those guardian seraphs, down among "The Islands," where he and the devil may do as they please.

"'Og!" observed the mate, as he passed through to the captain's cabin, and fetched out the sextant. "'Alf-caste or quarter-caste, Vaiti's too good a daughter for him, by the length of the mainmast and the mizzen together. She's got all his brains—Lord, how she learned navigation from him, like a cat lapping up milk, when she set her mind to it!—and none of his villainy. At least——" The mate paused on the companion, and filled his pipe.

"At least——" he repeated, and broke off the remark unfinished.

"Sun coming out nice now," he said, handing the sextant to the girl. Vaiti made her observation with the ease of an old sea-captain, and went below to work it out. It was true, as Harris said, that she had plenty of brains, though they did not lie along the lines of "The Maiden's Prayer" and Dr. Smith's English Grammar. And, whatever the legal status of poor derelict Saxon, or the mate, might be, no one who had ever climbed the side of the schooner *Sybil* could doubt the obvious fact that the real commanding officer of that vessel was Vaiti herself.

"What d'ye make it?" asked the mate, looking over her shoulder. Vaiti, always sparing of her words, pointed to the figures. Harris whistled.

"Ain't we off our course, just!" he said, drawing his finger down the chart.

"No," said Vaiti.

"Why, hang it all, Cap"—the girl was accorded the title, half in fun, half through habit, a good deal oftener than her father—"we ain't making for the Delgada reefs, are we? I don't pretend to be any navigator, but I do know the course for Papeëte."

"What you think not matter," said Vaiti, rolling up the chart. "Make him eight bell. You go take wheel; I ki-ki [dinner], then I take him."

"What's the course?" demanded the mate eagerly.

"Nor'-west by west," answered Vaiti, going into her cabin, and slamming the door against Harris's open-mouthed questions.

An Aitutaki boy with a chain of red berries in his hair, and a scarlet and yellow "pareo" (kilt) for all clothing, brought up the dinner. Vaiti ate her meal alone, and then came on deck to take over the wheel, keeping a determined silence that Harris hardly cared to break.... And yet—Nor'-west by west, with the wind fair for distant Papeëte, and the deadly Delgadas lying about a quarter point off their present course, not ten miles away!

"She's a hard case, bo'sun," he remarked to that official as they sat down together. "She has me fair scared with the course she's steering; and yet, you may sling me over the side in a shotted hammock for the sharks'es ki-ki, if she don't know a lot more than the old man himself. Ain't she a daisy, too! Look at her there 'olding the wheel, as upright as a cocoanut palm, and as pretty and plump as a—as a——"

"Porker," concluded the bo'sun, pouring an imperial pint of tea into his mug.

"You ain't got no poetry in you," said the mate disgustedly.

"Nor nothing else," growled the bo'sun. "Ain't you going to help that curry, and give a man something to put in his own inside after stowing the whale-boat full of beef and biscuits?"

"The whale-boat? (That's plenty, bo'sun; I've got to live as well as you)."

"Ay, biscuits, beef, and water; compass and sextant. She give the order a while ago."

"What's in the wind now?"

"I don't ask questions, so I'm never told no lies."

"I do, though," said the mate, in a spasm of authority, deserting his dinner to spring up the companion and join Vaiti at the wheel. The bo'sun's mahogany face broke up into a score of curving wrinkles, and his shoulders shook a little, as he watched the scene on deck. Quite mechanically he transferred the rest of the curry to his plate, and while clearing the dish with the precision of a machine, kept an eye on the couple at the wheel. He saw Harris ask an eager question, and repeat it more eagerly. He saw Vaiti jerk a brief answer, and the mate speak again. Then he saw the girl swing round on her heel, lift one slender hand, and bring it down across Harris's cheek with an emphasis that left a crimson mark upon the polished brown. He saw the mate take a step forward, and look at the handsome helmswoman as though he were very much minded to pay back the correction after the manner of man in general where a pretty vixen is concerned. The two figures stared at each other, eye to eye, for a full minute. Vaiti's brown eyes, keen as twin swords, never wavered; her lip was insolent and unrelenting. The mate's half-angry, half mischievous expression dissolved into an embarrassed grin; then he turned tail and hurried down the hatch.

"She's a tigress in 'uman form," he declared. "If the old man—or any other—was to lay 'is little finger on me—but there! who cares what a scratchin' cat does? I'd as soon marry a shark—I would!"

"You've as much chance," granted the bo'sun.

"Talk of sharks!" said the mate, gazing ruefully at the table and the empty dish.

Some two hours later, a milky gleam on the port bow attracted the mate's attention as he stood on the poop. A Kanaka sailor had just taken the wheel, and Vaiti was below.

"Breakers on the port bow!" sang out Harris.

Vaiti was up in a minute.

"I t'row water on my father's head," she said coolly—"but no good; he too much sick, he see snake by and by, I think. You and Oki carry him into him cabin, and come back pretty quick. I see this t'rough myself."

"See *what?*" demanded the mate, on the last verge of frenzy.

"Not know myself yet," answered Vaiti, giving one of her rare laughs. She seemed in a very good humour for once.

When the mate came out a little later, and the sailor went back to the neglected wheel, Vaiti was standing by the whale-boat, wearing an air of perfect self-possession and a complete suit of her father's white ducks. The sight was no novelty to Harris, but it came upon him now, as usually, with a new shock of admiration.

"Isn't she an outrighter!" he observed to the unsympathetic bo'sun.

"She certainly is, if outrighter's French for an undacent young woman," replied that officer sourly. Harris did not hear him, for the significance of the morning's mystery had just burst on his mind. He had not spent ten years in the Pacific for nothing and the sight of Tai, a diver from Penrhyn, standing beside Vaiti, with a water-glass in his hand, spelt "pearl-shell" to the eyes of the mate as clearly as if the magic word had been printed in letters three feet long. Vaiti flashed her white teeth at him.

"Tai, me, three boys, we go into lagoon," she said. "Suppose somethings happen, you find course for Apia written out, cabin table; you take ship back, put captain in hospital."

"By ——, but you're a corker, Vaiti!" cried Harris admiringly. "Where'd you hear anything about the Delgadas? No ship goes near them that can help it; they're a regular ocean cemetery."

"You 'member officer from gun-boat, Apia?"

"Ay!" said Harris. He did remember the lad, and the rather inexplicable friendliness shown him by Saxon and Vaiti during the stay in port of the *Alligator.*

"He show me photo Delgadas. *Alligator* he been go all round him, mark him right for chart, because he all wrong. Officer give my father bearings; say plenty talk and show photo. He dam fool officer, I think; he not know that kind place mean pearl-shell, and we not tell anything."

Harris mounted the rigging, and surveyed the reef from the main cross-trees. It was the best part of a mile away; a creaming circle of foam on the sea's blue surface, enclosing a pallid spot of green. Vaiti, who had followed him, flung one arm round the mast, and, leaning outwards towards the horizon, surveyed the reef intently. Within that ring of foam—the grave of many a gallant ship that had sailed the fair Pacific as bravely as their own little schooner—might lie many thousands of pounds. The repurchase of the *Sybil*, once Saxon's sole property, now partly owned by a trading syndicate; the regaining of her captain's lost position in decent society—perhaps the realisation of half a hundred luxurious dreams, dreamed on coral beaches under the romance-breeding splendours of the tropic moon—all this, and more, hung on the chances of the next few hours.

There was silence for the space of a minute or two, as the man and woman swung between earth and heaven, staring across the sun-dazzled plain of sea. Then, in one instant, the dream broke, and the rainbow fragments of that bubble of glory scattered themselves east and west. For across the bar of the level horizon slipped a small, pointed, pearl-coloured sail, growing as they watched it, flying past, and heading all too surely for the Delgadas reef.

Vaiti flung herself round a backstay, and slid down to the deck, with a word on her lips that would have justified the bo'sun's recent judgment, could he have caught it. Harris followed, swearing fully and freely. It was evident to both that the newcomer had special business with the reef as well as themselves; and they wasted no time, acting in concord, and without dispute, after a fashion that was new on board the *Sybil*. Within half an hour they had reduced the distance between the ship and the reef to a quarter of a mile; nearer than that even Vaiti did not care to go, for the weather looked unsettled, though the wind was off the reef. The whale-boat, with a picked crew, was lowered, and sent flying towards the break in the reef, while the mate, burning to be in her, but conscious that his duty must keep him on the ship, paced excitedly up and down the deck, glass in hand, watching the advance of the stranger ship from time to time. She was a good two hours' sail away as yet; and surely first possession was worth something, even out here in the lawless South Seas!

# CHAPTER II

## A RACE FOR A FORTUNE

Before an hour was over, the wind had freshened considerably, and the mate began to feel anxious for the safety of the boat, in case he should be obliged to run for it from the neighbourhood of the treacherous reef. That Vaiti would return an instant sooner because of the threatening weather he did not expect, knowing the dare-devil recklessness of her character too well. It was certain, however, that he might lose the ship, and incidentally himself, by waiting too long; and it was equally certain that Saxon, once recovered, would put a bullet through his mate's head if Vaiti came to harm. And all the time that threatening sail was growing larger and larger.

It was an unspeakable relief, though no less of a surprise, when he saw that the boat was actually heading towards the ship again, the sail up and every oar hard at work. He did not remember having seen Tai go down, in any of his hurried inspections through the glass, and the time was certainly short. What did it all mean?

The meaning became sufficiently clear as soon as the boat approached the ship, but not through the medium of eye or ear. A strong stench of rotting fish struck the mate's nostrils almost before the boat was within hail, and instantly enlightened him. No one who has ever smelt the terrible smell of the pearl-oyster removed from its ocean bed, and left to putrefy in a tropical sun, can mistake the odour. Harris understood at once that the strange ship had been there before, and that Vaiti was bringing back a sample of the last catch, left out to rot during the vessel's temporary absence.

The *Sybil* was leaping dangerously when the boat came alongside, but Vaiti snatched at the lowered rope, and swung herself up over the bulwarks before any of the native crew. Tai, following her, brought a sack of hideously smelling carrion, and dumped it down on the deck. The mate's eyes glistened.

"I find great lot lying on reef," said Vaiti, with an apparent calmness that might have deceived any one who knew her less accurately than the mate. "I think been there two week. C'lismas Island, he one week away, good weather. Papalangi C'lismas Island belong plenty diving gear. You see?"

"Rather!" said Harris gloomily. "Game up, eh?"

"I think you no man at all," spat Vaiti suddenly, swinging into the cabin. Harris, not especially put out, gave a hand to hauling in the boat, remarking to the bo'sun, who was picking over the heap of decaying pearl-shell, "Don't know as one could say the same about her, lump of solid devilment that she is! But this looks like the end of all our 'opes, as they say in the plays; don't it?"

In a minute or two Vaiti appeared again, wearing a dignified muslin gown with three frills on its tail, and holding a chart in her hands. She eyed the horizon narrowly, and ordered the ship to be put about, a manoeuvre which headed the *Sybil* straight for the oncoming sail. It was now evident that the stranger ship was a schooner of some eighty or ninety tons, rather larger than the *Sybil*, and nearly as fast. No one on board had the smallest doubt of her mission, even had that rotting heap of shell not been there to offer evidence. Pearl-shell lagoons, with their shell worth £100 to £200 per ton, and their pearls (if any are found, which is not always certain) worth a fortune for half a handful, are the gold mines of the South Sea world; the very birds of the sea seem at times to carry the news of such a discovery, and spread it far and wide.

The *Sybil* gathered way, and sped fast towards the stranger ship. The sea was blackening and rising, but there was not very much wind as yet. Vaiti sat cross-legged on the deck, studying her chart in the waning light of the gusty afternoon. It was some minutes before she laid it down and stood up to speak, steadying herself with one hand against the deck-house, for the schooner was now rolling heavily.

"Alliti," she said, "suppose you got heart one small fowl inside you, I get captain's Winchester, my levolver, you and bosun's levolver, and we send that people Davy Jones, or go ourself, pretty quick. But you not got heart, though you big man, and old man he all time sick. Now, you listen too much what I tell you. You run alongside ship, you go on board. You say captain sick, no one take sun, we get off course, nearly wreck on Delgadas. Then you ask captain give bearings reef, and you look at him chart too much careful, see if this line mark—here."

She put the point of her small forefinger on the chart she held, and showed two or three newly-ruled lines in red ink, enclosing a large space east and south of Samoa. These were the boundaries of the area lately annexed by New Zealand, and she was exceedingly anxious to know if the stranger knew as much about the significance of that matter as she did.

"Then," she went on, "you ask him if he been Wellington, say we wanting news——"

"What the (adjective noun) for?" demanded the mate.

"Because I say, pauki!" (pig) flashed Vaiti. "No!—you got head of pig, heart of fowl. You bo'sun, you know I get you through this all right, suppose you trusting me—you come here."

Harris, shaking his great shoulders in an easy laugh, swung down on to the main deck, and began ordering about the crew. He had an enormous admiration for Vaiti, even when she boxed his ears, but he thought her special peculiarities of character rather a trying obstacle in the way of his enjoying the easy life beloved of South Sea mates.

The acidulous bo'sun rose from his seat on deck, holding out an unclean palm, in the midst of which glittered two fine pearls.

"I've been through that little lot, and got these, which do look like biz, ma'am," he observed. "As to people havin' fowls' hearts, or pigs' heads, I'm not prepared to pass judgment. But I don't own to neither myself, and if you say it's a fight, a fight it is. Or if you've got a better plan in that uncommon level 'ead of yours, I'm ready to stand by."

"You something like a man," pronounced the commanding officer in the muslin skirt. "You listen. I tell him all again."

$$* \quad * \quad * \quad * \quad *$$

An hour later the bo'sun, very wet and draggled, climbed over the bulwarks of the *Sybil*, and the schooner *Margaret Macintyre*, of Sydney, slipped behind into the falling dusk.

"Said he was thirteen weeks out from Sydney, ma'am," reported the ambassador. "Four weeks out from Apia, gettin' copra round here and there, and there wasn't no Wellington news anywhere, as he remembered. Nice new chart, with no lines of that kind ruled on it anywhere. As to where he got the divin' gear that was in the cabin, or what kind of copra he reckoned to pick up on the Delgadas, he didn't say, not bein' asked."

Vaiti stood still to consider, a beautifully poised black silhouette against the yellow oblong of the lamp-lit cabin door.

"I think it all right; he not been near Wellington," she pronounced at last. "Alliti! How her head?"

"Sou'-west by south," answered the mate from the wheel.

"Keep her so."

"Ay, ay, sir!" laughed the mate.

$$* \quad * \quad * \quad * \quad *$$

Every one in the South Pacific knew that the *Sybil* was a marvel of speed, and that she had not been originally built for trading, though nobody could tell exactly how Saxon had acquired such a clipper. It was a popular theory that she was a millionaire's yacht from San Francisco, which he had stolen and subsequently disguised. He was known, however, to have possessed her for more than twenty years, and was now as completely identified with her as her own mainmast; so that any doubts as to the honesty of the way by which he might originally have obtained her were now of a purely academic nature.

Famous as she was for speed, the record of her passage from the Delgadas to Wellington fairly astonished the Islands, when it came to be told. They had a fair wind almost all the way, with two or three lively nights when the little vessel, hard driven under the utmost pressure of the canvas, piled up the knots like a liner. Saxon continued delirious, but was fortunately quiet. Harris, and Gray the boatswain, though unenlightened as to the cause of the *Sybil's* sudden southward flight, fully understood that the possession of the pearl lagoon hung in the balance, and worked like half-a-dozen to supplement the efforts of the scanty Kanaka crew.

Vaiti interfered little with the working of the ship, but she kept a look-out that hardly left her time for sleep or food; although the *Sybil*, like most Pacific ships, was allowed, under ordinary circumstances, to chance it, day and night. Hour after hour she sat cross-legged on deck, watching the unbroken rim of the black horizon, or paced up and down the poop, silent and grave, in her lace and muslin fripperies, as a naval officer on the bridge. What she was looking for no one knew, but during that wild ten days of foam and smother, cracking sails and straining sheets, her silent watchfulness infected the men themselves, and eyes were constantly turned to scan the empty, seething plain over which they flew.

It was drawing on towards dusk of the tenth day, and the sky was beginning to light fires of angry copper-purple, high in the storm-driven west, when Vaiti, of a sudden, stopped dead in her endless walk, and looked with lips apart and eyes narrowed deep beneath her brows over the weather rail. All this time they had not sighted a single sail or a solitary funnel. They had been well off the track of New Zealand bound ships, and the Pacific waters are wide. But now they were drawing near to Wellington, and there was nothing to be astonished at in the sight of another sail creeping up over the horizon, except, indeed, the fact that it was momentarily growing larger and gaining on the *Sybil*. There was scarce another schooner afloat from New Guinea to the Paumotus that could have done as much.

The mate came up behind Vaiti, and handed her a glass. She looked through it, lowered it, raised it, and looked again with a steady gaze, and suddenly flung it out of her hand across the deck.

Harris caught it deftly and asked, with the constitutional calm that alone saved his reason when Vaiti took over command, "What's to pay now?"

"She got auxiliary," said Vaiti, with a note of agony in her voice.

"What if she has? Isn't any vessel free to carry an auxiliary that can stand the stink of the oil and the cussedness of the injin?"

"I go see captain," said Vaiti, flashing down the companion.

Saxon was better to-day, and almost in full possession of his senses. Vaiti went to the medicine chest; took out a hypodermic syringe, filled it with careful accuracy from a tiny dark blue bottle, and lifted her father's arm as he lay limp and weak, but mending fast, in his bunk.

"Good girl, take care of your old father," he murmured in island Maori as she slipped the needle-point painlessly under the skin, and the powerful drug began to race through every vein of the inert body. The effect was rapid and decisive. Saxon sat up against his pillows in five minutes, clear-headed though weak, and asked if the *Sybil* had not sighted the Delgadas yet.

"Listen, father," said Vaiti, speaking fluently in the low, soft tongue that the two had used together all her life—the Maori language Saxon had first learned from the pretty brown girl, dead this many years, whom he had stolen from her South Sea island to sail the blue Pacific at his side in the days of long ago. "Listen. There is little time, and we are in great need. We came to the reef, and the shell was there truly, but a strange ship had been before us. Even as we lay there she returned from Christmas Island with diving gear. I sent Gray on board to look at her chart and find out if she had been to Wellington; and it seemed that she had not the new line of annexation marked on the chart, where New Zealand this year added to herself all that lay within a certain space of the sea; also she had not been south of Auckland. So then, knowing that we, if we asked the Government, might have the atoll granted us for twenty years and take possession above the people of the other ship, I made sail for Wellington; and we are now but one day away when this ship appears again, chasing us. Where the suspicion has waked in their hearts, or when, is nothing; but that they have thought and discovered our desire, that is certain."

"Give the *Sybil* all sail, daughter, and she will leave the other. What is this talk?" asked Saxon, raising himself on his elbow to look out of the glooming circle of the port.

"But the ship has 'auxiliary,' my father, and she will have passed out of sight before the morning."

"Oh, she has, has she?" grunted the captain, dropping back into his native tongue. "What are you going to do about it?"

He had noted a glimmer in Vaiti's eye that told him that she was not yet at the end of her resources. The Maori guile and the English daring were united to some purpose in this strange creature that he had given to the world.

"I will tell," she said, standing up to her full height. "But you must give the order, my father, for Alliti drags on the rein these days. Let the bale of trawl-net, and the Manila rope, be taken from the cargo, and let us cross the bows of this ship, and drop them across her path. The keel will run clean, but the screw will foul, and they will creep like a bird with a broken wing till daylight. Then, if the sea has grown less, they will send down a diver and clear the screws; but we shall be almost into Wellington, and the lagoon is ours."

"You are worthy to be the daughter of a brave man," answered Saxon in Maori, sinking back wearily on his pillow. "Go, then; and if we lose the ship, we lose her; there is great wealth to gain, and a man must die at one time, if not another. I am tired. I will sleep."

Vaiti left him, and hurried back on deck. The purple dusk was already beginning to gather, and the green starboard light of the *Margaret Macintyre* gleamed like a glow-worm a mile or so behind. She was drawing very near; there was no time to lose.

"Alliti!" called Vaiti. "My father he better; he send word to take trawl-net and Malila out of hold, make come across that ship him path, foul him sclew. Suppose you not afraid, you bring us close, drop net and Malila."

Harris's hide was thick, but Vaiti knew how to pierce it when she chose; and the man had courage enough, in streaks. Vaiti had hit the mark when she called him chicken-hearted in fighting, but there was no manoeuvre of the ship too risky for him to undertake and carry through with perfect coolness.

"All right, my lady," he nodded. "Don't forget me and Gray when it comes to sharing out the swag, that's all."

The net and the rope were brought up, and the latter knotted here and there to make a hideous tangle of it. Then the *Sybil's* lights were put out, even the cabin lamp being extinguished. The stars pricked themselves out in sudden sharpness on the great blue chart of heaven above, and the waste of dark rolling water all around grew large and lonely.

You are not to suppose that Saxon's daughter did not see and feel these things—did not hear the voiceless talk of the great seas on starry evenings, or feel her mortal body almost rapt away in the ecstasy of a black midnight and a shrieking storm; just as you, perhaps, who think that no one ever shared such experiences with yourself, may feel. It is not only the blameless tourist, with his daily diary, and his books of travel teaching him how and when to "enthuse," who enjoys the splendid pageant of the seas. Vaiti, as the most indulgent chronicler must confess, had more than a spice of her father's villainy in her composition, not to speak of whatever devilry her Maori forebears might have bequeathed to her. She was unscrupulous, ruthless, and crafty as a general rule; she was engaged in a deed of the very shadiest description to-night—yet, as she stood with her hands on the wheel, and her eyes on the green starboard light of the oncoming ship, steering the *Sybil* to something extremely like certain destruction, she knew that the Southern Cross was rising, clear and beautiful, above its gem-like pointers, just ahead;

and that a little sliver of young moon, crystal-silver against the dark, was slipping up the sky to her left. The thought just grazed her mind that this might be the last time the moon would ever rise over the Pacific for her. She smiled a little in the dusk, and steered steadily ahead. There were no "streaks" in the composition of Vaiti's spirit.

A short tack to the starboard became necessary. Harris put the ship about at a lift of Vaiti's hand. It grew very dark; a cloud was over the moon, and the stars were dimmed by driving vapour. The wind was increasing; the schooner lay over with its weight, and the foam gurgled along her clean-ran sides. Still the *Margaret Macintyre* came on, stately and unsuspicious, all sail set, and the beat of the little screw distinctly audible through the night.

Vaiti signalled again to put the ship about, and as soon as the great booms had creaked across the deck, gave over the wheel to Harris.

"Run him just as he head now," she said softly, "and bring him too much close; so (double adjective) close to ship he scrape the (qualified) paint off him. I go do rest."

Harris, humming "Good-bye, Dolly Gray," took the wheel over. If he had any doubts as to Vaiti's purpose, the vigour of her language would have dispersed them. Vaiti never swore unless she was exceedingly in earnest.

The trawl-net and the tangle of Manila were hanging over the stern, held up by a single rope. Vaiti glided to the rail, holding a sharp knife in her hand— ("I always *did* think she kept one somewhere among her frilligigs," commented Harris silently, as he caught the flash of the steel)—and waited, still as a statue.

Presently out of the darkness shot a hail, accompanied by a perfect constellation of oaths. Its apparent object was to ascertain the *Sybil's* reason for steering such a course. The *Sybil* answered not a word, but steered the course some more.

The hail, at the second time of repeating, became a yell, with a strong note of terror in it. On came the *Sybil*, a dim, unlit tower of blackness, taking as much notice of the shouts as the *Flying Dutchman*. Those on board the *Margaret Macintyre* gave themselves up for lost. There was even a rush made for one of the boats. But the threatening shape swept past her bows, so near that the furious captain could have tossed a biscuit on board—so near that the *Sybil's* Kanaka crew, thinking the "papalangi" officers meant to ram the stranger, uttered war-cries wherein pure delight was mingled with overjoyed surprise.

It was all over in a minute, and the *Sybil* was well away on the *Margaret Macintyre's* port side before the latter vessel discovered, through the medium of a horrible jar from the engine-room and a powerful odour of oil, that the screw was badly fouled, leaving them, like St. Paul with nothing to do but make the best of circumstances, and "wish that it were day."

*　　*　　*　　*　　*

December weather is hot in Wellington, and it was now close to Christmas. Perhaps that was why the senior member of the trading firm that had taken over part ownership of the *Sybil* for an unpaid debt thought his eyes were deceived by the glare of the sun when he saw a white schooner of singularly graceful lines lying alongside one of the wharves on a date when her engagements plainly demanded her presence in Tahiti.

When, however, he met Saxon and his daughter, a few minutes afterwards, on Lambton Quay, he understood that his eyes were in excellent order. So, it soon appeared, was his tongue. He was a gentleman of Scottish extraction, and it hurt him badly to see possible profits thrown away.

Saxon let him have his say, and merely laughed for answer.

"Come into the Occidental, and Vaiti and I'll tell you something worth all the trade that you'd take out of Papeëte in ten years," he said. "I'm going to own the ship again before New Year's Day, and paint this good old town scarlet as well. You'll see."

And the man of money-bags, anxious to see, went into the hotel.

Vaiti, in a fit of perversity, declined to come in. She knew only too well that, in Saxon's impecunious condition, there was no hope of getting their discovery effectively worked save at a price that would leave very little change over for the present possessors of the lagoon—even if the captain had been quite sober, which he was not. They had got the grant, and had furthermore had the satisfaction of noting that, day after day, Wellington Harbour remained empty of the hardly-used *Margaret Macintyre*. It was evident that her people, whoever they were, had tamely accepted defeat. There was no standing against a grant from the Government of New Zealand—no matter how acquired. But all this did not alter the fact that there was not going to be a great deal for the *Sybil*, and her captain, and her captain's daughter— especially the latter. It was there that the sting lay. Vaiti had had dreams— oh, but dreams! oh, such dreams! before solid common-sense had brought her down to earth, and made her realise that Saxon's unlucky state, and the eminently Scottish firm who held the destinies of the *Sybil* in their hands, were quite certain to stand in the way of realisation. To make a fortune, you must first have one, generally speaking. And it was the canny Glasgow men who had it.

So, because she did not want to hear with her own ears what she knew very well must take place, she refused to come into the hotel, and wandered off alone down the quays, in the warm December sun, which yet was cool compared to the burning heats of the island world. She was dressed in a long, waistless muslin gown, as usual, but her shady Niué hat and white deck shoes—not to speak of a pair of kid gloves that caused her horrible discomfort and a parasol that embarrassed her extremely—spoke of a respect for certain of the conventions that might have astonished people who knew, or thought they knew, Vaiti of the Islands. Of course, the loungers on the quays looked admiringly after her—she would have liked to see them dare to omit that tribute to her fiery charms—and some of them freely spoke to her, calling her Mary and Polly, offering her hearts and drinks and new bonnets, and asking her for kisses or jobs on the schooner, just as it occurred to them, after the simple fashion of the sea. Some of them knew her, and some of them did not. It was the latter who asked for jobs. The men who did know the *Sybil* and her "Kapitani" asked for kisses, which they did not expect to get. That was safer.

Vaiti, quite accustomed to this sort of demonstration, and enjoying it in a languid way as she strolled along under the annoying parasol, covered half a mile or so of the quay at her own leisurely pace, and then sat down on a coil of rope in a quiet place, to stare across the water and think.

She wanted something, and she did not see her way to get it.

To disentangle the dreams and hopes, wild fancies, and wilder aspirations of the half-caste mind when that mind, puzzling and elusive enough to the pure white in any case, is further complicated with a touch of genius, would be a task worthy of a whole academy of science. This much alone can the necessarily all-knowing biographer of Vaiti say—that she wanted to be someone, and wanted it so badly that nothing else in life seemed worth having, or even existent, She was a princess of Atiu on her mother's side, and on her father's (though Saxon's past was as much a mystery as the origin of the yacht-like *Sybil* herself) Vaiti felt that she had every right to claim high standing.

Doubly dowered, therefore, with the instinct of rule, the actual command of the schooner had fallen into her capable hands quite naturally. Left to herself, she would probably have made the *Sybil* pay in a way unknown before to the easy-going island world. But the useless, dissipated Saxon had to be counted on. She liked him in her own way, such as it was, but she despised him also. And it was an undoubted fact that he hampered everything. This bargain with M'Coy and Co., for instance—it was useless for her to attempt to put a finger on it. Saxon had got drunk the night before, as soon as the matter of the grant had been finally decided, at the end of some anxious days of waiting;

and in the morning the numerous "hairs" that he had taken to restore him had left him in a condition of hopeless obstinacy and self-sufficiency. In such a state he was as certain to be over-reached as a stranded jelly-fish is certain to be licked up by the sun. And this was bitter to Vaiti.

For, sitting there motionless under the parasol (which was serving a useful purpose at last, in shading her handsome face from observation and comment by the passers-by), Vaiti had arrived at something rather like a conclusion, and a conclusion, too, that was likely to shape most of her thoughts and acts henceforward.

Money was the thing.

She did not care for money in itself, and none of the things it could bring really interested her, except pretty clothes.

But money was importance, money was power; money was the freedom to do exactly what you wanted, and make other people do it too. She did not think it out in words, like a European. Pictures passed before her mind, more vivid by far than the glittering water and flashing sea-gull wings in front of her bodily eyes. She saw captains of great ships, giving orders like kings, and obeyed by the promptest and smartest of slaves. She saw owners of big stores entertaining half the island on their verandahs, paid court to by wandering beach-combers, going out to ships in beautiful boats manned by their own uniformed crews, who bent their backs double at a word. She saw "Tusitala," of Samoa, the great English story-teller, living in his splendid house outside Apia, surrounded by a humble clan of native followers wearing wonderful lava-lavas of a foreign stuff they called "tatani" (tartan)—Tusitala, who was as great a chief as Mataafa himself, and had spoken to her, Vaiti, as one worthy of all honour.... Her pictures were almost all of the islands, for the islands were in her blood; but something, too, she saw of Auckland—the merchant M'Coy, old and so ugly, and of the commonest birth, yet reverenced like the greatest of chiefs, because he had money....

The afternoon rays grew blinding hot on the water as the sun sank down. The sea-gulls dipped and screamed. Steamers glided away from the wharves with long hooting cries that somehow seemed to embody all the melancholy of the homeless sea. Steam cranes chattered ceaselessly above the yawning holds of discharging ships. Behind, the tramcars hummed in the street, and people hurried up and down.

And at last the western sky began to burn with sultry red, and Vaiti went home.

Something had taken root in her mind that afternoon that struck down and shot up, in the days to come, and led her into ways and places wilder even than the adventure of the pearl lagoon. As children string berries on a straw, so upon the stem that grew from that seed were strung the strange events that followed, one by one.

# CHAPTER III

## THE FLOWER BEHIND THE EAR

As Vaiti, Cassandra-wise, had prophesied about the pearl lagoon, so indeed it fell out.

It takes money to exploit even the smallest discovery of this kind, and the canny M'Coy made the most of the fact. Delgadas Reef was too risky a neighbourhood to be worked by any vessel unprovided with an auxiliary engine, so a cranky little schooner of some forty tons, owning a tiny oil engine that sometimes worked and sometimes did not—more commonly the latter—was chartered; also a couple of boats for diving work, and two sets of diving dresses; and a cheap crew was picked up somewhere, and some poor provisions laid in. Everything was done on the most economical scale possible—yet the Scotchman grumbled and lamented, and declared he would never see his money back. The shares had been fixed at a wickedly low figure for Saxon and there were, furthermore, clauses in the agreement concerning expenses which made that unlucky derelict swear fiercely when he read them after he was sober. It was too late to complain then, however, for he had signed everything he was asked, under the influence of the good whisky to which M'Coy—liberal for once—had freely treated him. Nor did he get any sympathy from Vaiti. She merely laughed when he complained, and told him frankly that he would have done better to stay in his cabin and drink there, if he liked, leaving her to finish what she had begun.

So the pearling ship sailed off, and Saxon, who could not afford to stay in port, went another voyage. And some months later, when he came back, it was to find that Delgadas Reef was cleaned out. It had held not much after all, said the Glasgow man, and shell was down, and the pearls had been few and off colour. But there was enough to pay Saxon's debt and leave him owner and master of the *Sybil* once more. And there might be a few pounds in addition—not much; but there, he was an honest man, and he would rather ruin himself than let Saxon and the charming Miss Vaiti feel they were badly treated. And if Saxon would kindly sign this paper releasing him from all further claims, he would be happy to give over all claim in the ship. Otherwise—money was tight, and that little matter between them had been owing so long that——

Saxon interrupted with a statement to the effect that he knew blank well he had been blank well had, and for the sum of two sanguinary sixpences he would be prepared to knock Mr. M'Coy's doubly condemned head off his unpleasantly qualified shoulders—only, luckily for Mr. M'Coy, he was sick of him and the like of him, and merely wanted to get out of his way as soon as he possibly could. With which concise summing up of facts he signed the paper, picked up the cheque, and went out to spend it after his own fashion. Vaiti secured half of it at the bank where he cashed it, and went off with the money done up in her hair, to keep house by herself on the schooner until her father should turn up again. She knew him too well to expect that that would come about immediately.

Meanwhile, there were banks in which she could deposit her own share, and thus feel herself a step nearer to her goal—that dim, undefined goal that was to be reached somehow, some time, through the possession of the precious bits of paper and coin without which all pleasant things were impossible. She did not decide at once where the money should go, but hid it in her cabin, and day by day walked the pavements of Wellington, delighting her eyes with the shop-window beauties which she had so seldom seen. Thus came her undoing. Vaiti had never heard the saying, "We are none of us infallible, even the youngest," or she might have been less certain of herself before it came about, and less bitter afterwards.

For was it not natural that when Saxon unexpectedly reappeared at the Constantinople Hotel with a good deal of his money still left, and sent for Vaiti to join him and "live like a lady while she could," the improvident island blood should all unbidden well up and smother everything else? Why go on? There are shops in Wellington—there are as many ways of getting fifteen shillings' worth out of a sovereign, and repeating the process a great deal oftener than one means, as in any other of the world's big ports.... The end was that, after ten delirious days of glorious spending, Captain Saxon and his daughter set sail for Tahiti with a general cargo, a complete set of empty pockets between them, and, on the part of Vaiti, a glad remembrance more than half stifled by angry regret for the cost. Yet, and yet, what a lovely thing money was, and what a pity that one could not both spend and keep it! If you did the one, you were happy, but no one thought anything of you. If you did the other, everyone paid court to you, but you didn't get the fun. Yes, that was true of money—and of other things. Girls who had been brought up at convent schools understood a lot that the ignorant beach girls didn't.... And, *bon Dieu!* as they used to say in Papeëte, when the Sisters couldn't hear—what a headache it gave her to think, and what a fool she was to do it!

"Ruru!" she called in Maori to a native sleeping peacefully on the deck. "Wake up, pig-face, son of a fruit-bat, and make me kava immediately. I am weary."

\* \* \* \* \*

It was many weeks after, and the hot season had come round once more.

The schooner was slamming helplessly about on a huge glassy swell. Everything on board that could rattle, rattled; everything in the cabins that could break loose and take charge, did so, sending up a melancholy chorus of crashes with every wallow of the ship. The great mizzen sail slatted about above the poop, offering and then instantly withdrawing a promise of cooling shade, in a manner that was little short of maddening, seeing that the hour was three o'clock, and the latitude not four degrees south. Friday Island looking like a small blue flower on the rim of a crystal dish, hovered tantalisingly on the extreme verge of the horizon, as unattainable as Sydney Heads or heaven. For the *Sybil* was becalmed, a week's from anywhere in particular, and there seemed no chance of a breeze.

"Lord," said the mate, dropping the marlinspike with which he was splicing a rope, and mopping his forehead with his rolled-up sleeve, "I wonder 'ow many thousand miles we are from an iced beer!"

"Turtle!" said Vaiti, taking a slim brown cigar out of her mouth, and looking down from her seat on the top of the deck-house. "Only nine hundred and eighty-seven. You not remember Charley's in Apia?"

"I'd forgotten Samoa," said Harris, in a more cheerful tone, picking up the marlinspike, and going to work again, as if revived by Vaiti's arithmetic.

"A miss is as good as a mile, for all me, specially when it's nine hundred mile," remarked the gloomy boatswain. "Couldn't you manage to talk about something rather less 'arrowing to a man's insides?"

"I'd like to know why she's going skull-huntin' to Friday Island, then," said the mate, casting a cautious glance at Vaiti, who was scarcely out of ear-shot, up on the deck-house.

"Trade I can understand," he went on, "and shell-huntin'—we haven't done too bad all round over that last little job, and the old man's a sight more sober since he's owned the ship again. But skulls—and old skulls at that—filthy natives' bones that's been lyin' in the caves since Heaven knows when! Besides, they ain't our skulls, however you may look at it——"

"Nor I hope they won't be," said the boatswain darkly. "In no way, I mean. The Friday Islanders aren't people to ask out to an afternoon tea-party without you've got your knuckle-duster on underneath your voylet kid gloves. And you know what natives are about their old bones and graves."

"I do. What I don't know is how she thinks she's going to make anything out of a proper nasty job like that."

"Oh, she's on the make, is she!"

"Did you ever know her anything else, bless her?" asked the mate. "She wants sixty pounds, havin' spent all the old man give her out of the shell business in Wellington, takin' boxes at the theaytres and halls, and buyin' women's gear, and staying at the Constantinople, where she wore two new 'ats a day for a week; and other games of a similar kind. Pity you was sick, and not there to see the fun. I tell you, she made the town look silly."

"What's the sixty pound for?" asked the boatswain, chewing fondly on his quid.

Harris giggled explosively, and whispered:

"She wants a Dozey dress!"

"What in ——'s that? It don't sound respectable," virtuously observed the boatswain, who had never heard of the famous French dressmaker.

"You bet it is, then. Dozey's a regular bang-up swell in Paris, who makes the most expensive gownds in the world, and every one in them parts treats him just the same as a baronight or a duke. You can't get so much as a jumper from him for less than sixty pound, and Vaiti she says every woman in Papeëte or Aucklan' or Sydney who saw one of his dresses would spot it right away, and go and throw herself over the Heads. She read about his things in a piece in one of them female papers in the hotel, and she saw an actress wearin' of one, and she's been layin' out to get one ever since, somethin' awful. Seems when a woman in London, or Paris, or Yarmouth gets a Dozey dress, and takes to standin' off and on before the others, who's only got new velveteens with musling frills or such-like it just makes them other women drag their anchors and run head-on to the shore. So Vaiti, she——"

"Hold on," interrupted the boatswain. "Why, if she 'ad one of those gownds, she couldn't bend it on to her yards, not if it cost a million. Man alive, she ain't laid down on the same lines as them Frenchwomen, anyway."

"You let her alone for that," chuckled Harris. "But what beats me is *who* she's going to do with them skulls, and *how*. We won't know in a hurry, either, because she and Pita's fixed it up between them to do the job alone. Thank 'eaven for small mercies, says I. 'Er on the war-path's rather more than I care for; and this isn't going to be any picnic, if I know anything of natives."

"Pita!" whistled the boatswain. "The old man will 'ave 'is gore before the voyage is out, if Vaiti goes on like this. It's Ritter, that fat German trader in Papeëte, that he's wanting to marry her to; and as for natives, it's 'ands off for them, if she is 'alf of one 'erself."

"Well, she and Pita was planning it all out in the fore-top last night. I heard them, when she thought I was sleeping on the top of the galley. And the old man came out and roared at her like a Marquesas bull to come down; so down she came, laughing at him, like the devil she is. There's no one else on this ship would laugh, without it was on the wrong side of his mouth, when the old man gets ratty. Coming! All right!"

The mate jumped to his feet, and answered Vaiti's sharp hail in person, a deprecating smile spreading like spilt treacle all over his face as he came up to her, cap in hand. Vaiti took her cigar out of her mouth, and looked at him for a minute without speaking. The *Sybil* rolled on the towering swell like a captured beast trying to beat its brains out against a wall, but Saxon's Maori daughter stood as steady as the slender main-mast upon the reeling deck. Harris smiled more than ever, and turned the marlinspike about in his hands, looking a little foolish.

"You wanting Captain Saxon come and lay you out in the scupper pretty soon?" inquired Vaiti presently.

"Not particular," answered the mate, the smile sliding slowly off his face.

"Then I think perhaps you keep your mouth more better shut," said Vaiti, walking off with a contemptuous swing in the very fall of her laced muslin skirts. And Pita of Atiu, as if in defiance of the captain, the mate, and every one else but his cousin Vaiti, pulled a mouth-organ out of his shirt and began to play it triumphantly and frantically, making a noise exactly like the buzzing of a mad bluebottle on a warm window-pane. Further, he plucked a frangipani flower out of the wreath—a good deal the worse for wear—that hung round his neck, and stuck the blossom behind his ear. Now, every one who has ever been in the Islands knows that these two actions are significant of courtship. Pita was courting Vaiti, as everybody knew—Pita, a mere deck hand, who had been taken on at wild Atiu, in the Cook Islands, because he was a relation of Saxon's dead native wife. Very handsome was Pita, very young and tall and broad-shouldered, wily and fierce like all the Atiuans, but smooth and pleasant of countenance. Were not the men of Atiu nicknamed "meek-faced Atiuans," even in the days, only a generation gone, when they were the cruellest and most warlike of cannibals and pirates?

Needless to say, Captain Saxon, who had always had "views" for Vaiti, ever since she left the Tahitian convent school that had given her such fragments of civilisation as she possessed, did not favour the compromising attentions of Pita. As for Vaiti, her father's prohibitions neither piqued her into noticing the handsome Atiuan more, nor alarmed her into favouring him less, than she found agreeable. At present there was rather more than less about the matter, because Saxon was in one of his fits of gloomy depression, and Vaiti foresaw the usual result. It was not at all likely that her father would be able to help her in her forthcoming raid. Harris she did not choose to rely on at a pinch; Gray was old; the crew were far and away too superstitious to aid in such a sacrilege as she proposed. There remained Pita, who, if he was a wild Atiuan, was at least "misinari" after a fashion, had been educated, more or less, in Raratonga, and was most certainly in love with herself.... Yes, Pita would do.

That night, when the second dog-watch had commenced, and a few large crystal stars were just beginning to glimmer through the pink of the ocean sunset, Vaiti descended to the cabin, looked into Gray and Harris's berths to make sure that they were both on deck, and then sat down on the cushioned locker opposite her father.

"What is it?" asked Saxon, raising his heavy blue eyes. He had been sitting with his head propped in the corner of the cabin, silent as a fish, since the clearing away of tea an hour before. You might have thought him asleep, or, if you knew him intimately, drunk. He was neither; but dead and drowned things were rising up from the black sea caverns of his heart to-night, and their bones showed white and ghastly upon the desert shores of his life. So he sat silent, with his face turned to the darkening porthole and to the night that was striding down upon the sea.

Through the port he saw the shining harbour of Papeëte as it looked a week or two ago—a tall grey British war-ship lying at anchor, the *Sybil's* dinghy, small and crank and unclean, creeping up to the man-of-war's accommodation-ladder, himself, a weather-scarred, red-faced figure, in a worn duck suit and bulging shoes, sitting in the boat, and waiting patiently until the Governor's steam-launch should have passed in front of him and discharged its freight of visitors.

He saw the captain of the great Queen's ship standing at the top of the ladder, slight and trig and trim, all white and gold from top to toe, all smiling self-possession and cool command.

He saw ladies, immaculately coiffed and daintily shod; tall, clean, grey-moustached men following them; a cordial welcome on the deck; a flutter of light drapery and a glimpse of lounging masculine figures afterwards, framed by the great open gun-ports of the captain's cabin in the stern. They were laughing and talking, and he could hear the clink of cups and glasses. After— a long time after—he could see his own shabby little boat creeping up to the ladder; the captain, cold and business-like, and more than a little brusque, speaking to him on the deck about a certain anchorage in the Cook Islands group, concerning which he was known to have information; himself, burningly conscious of his shoes and his finger-nails, answering shortly and with some embarrassment, and feeling, of a sudden, very shabby, very broken, very old.... Was it twenty-five years, or two thousand, since the Admiral of the Fleet, and the Prince of Saxe-Brandenburg, with half the mess of his own regiment, had dined on board his biggest yacht at Cowes a week before—it—happened? ... Now a mere commander left him standing on the deck, and spoke to him like a native or a dog. Well, what did it all matter to a dead man? Was not his name of those days carved on the family monument in letters half an inch deep, and was not he, Edward Saxon, whom nobody knew, out here in the living death of the farthermost islands, a thousand miles from anywhere? ...

"Father," said Vaiti.

"What is it?" answered Saxon's voice dully, as befitted a dead man.

"The wind is rising at last," said the girl in Maori, "We shall be off the island by morning. Will you, or will you not, go with me into this cave of death, where I have told you that I shall find what is worth finding?"

"I have no heart. I will not."

"Then I and Pita will go," said Vaiti, fixing the Englishman's blue eyes with her own black, stabbing and savagely unfathomable, yet set in Saxon's very own narrow high-bred face.

The captain's dark mood was on him, and he turned his face to the wall, with a Maori oath consigning Vaiti and Pita to a cannibal end.

"I go; stay you there," said Vaiti, using the quaintly courteous native form of farewell, barbed with a little sneer unknown to the original. Then she went to her cabin. And Saxon turned in his seat, and reached for the brandy bottle at last.

*　　*　　*　　*　　*

Handsome Pita had a great awe for Vaiti, for she was a princess of Atiu by her mother's side. But she was beautiful, and he admired her—also he hoped that her imperious soul harboured one soft spot for him. It seemed good, on the whole, when they were pulling the dinghy over the reef next morning, to ask Vaiti openly where the value of the booty came in—with a secret hope in the background of securing as much as possible for a certain very deserving, more or less Christian youth of Atiu.

Vaiti, her white dress girded up high over her scarlet pareo, waded through the last yard or two of the emerald lagoon before she answered. The boat being safe on shore, she stood up and looked sharply about her. They had chosen a quiet spot at the back of the island for landing, all the natives being down at the harbour loading copra. The weird pandanus trees, standing on their high wooden stilts at the verge of the shore, the rustling coco-palms swinging their great fronds far over the water, the golden and pink-flowered vines trailing yard on yard of green garlandry over the paper-white sand, could carry no tales, and they were the only witnesses.

Vaiti looked at Pita up and down, from head to foot, and Pita gave the flower behind his ear a knowing cock, and set one hand saucily on his hip. He knew that he was the handsomest man in the Cook archipelago, and he felt that the way his pareo was tied that day was a pure inspiration. So he shut up his mouth very tight, and made play with his burning black eyes as only a South Sea Islander can, waiting confidently the while for the information that the whole ship's company of the *Sybil* could not have extracted from Vaiti in a week.

The girl stepped forward, and with a commanding finger tapped Pita's biggest dimple, as if he had been a baby.

"Suppose I tell you, then you know too much, you plenty frighten, go back to ship," she laughed.

"Speak Maori, high chieftainess!" implored Pita.

"No fee-ah!" answered Saxon's daughter succinctly. Pita understood at once that Vaiti was unwilling to use a language that gave free rein to her tongue and his, and the knowledge elated him.

"Perhaps I tell you," went on Vaiti, watching him narrowly. "I think you got heart in belly belong you, more better than Alliti. I tell you, you want plenty heart by-and-by."

"High chieftainess, Vaiti, speak Maori!" was Pita's answer, linked to an attempted embrace that only fell short of its main object because Vaiti quite calmly pulled a seaman's knife out of her dress and laid it edge upwards across her lips. Pita, who had learned the real European kiss during his visits to civilisation, and wanted very much to show it off, felt disappointed, although there was a smile behind the blade that almost out-dazzled the steel.

"Maori!" he persisted, putting his arm round her waist, with a cool disregard of her well-known readiness with the knife that won Vaiti's admiration a step further than before. She laughed, wavered, and then, still playing with the keen, bright blade, she lowered it a little, and spoke in the soft language of the Islands at last.

It was a fairly long tale that she had to tell. When last the *Sybil* had been in the Society Islands, some weeks before, there had been a German man of science in the group, collecting native skulls for museums at home. The grizzly old gentleman and his pursuits had not troubled Vaiti's mind particularly until her chief admirer, Ritter, a Papeëte trader, happened to drop a remark one day about the amount of money some of these old skulls were worth. Vaiti's sharp intelligence linked on the casual saying at once to certain other wandering rumours she remembered, and she decided to find out something more. She did not ask Ritter, for he was no talker, even to a handsome girl whom he admired; and the German was his compatriot, in any case. But when the schooner reached Raiatea, where Professor Spricht was staying, Vaiti drifted off among the native huts, and squatted for an hour or two on the mats of the second chief's wife's mother's cousin's house, smoking a great deal, talking very little, and listening quietly. By degrees the house filled up with interested natives all eager for gossip and chatter; and to Vaiti, pulling steadily at her cigar, and maintaining the grave, unsmiling demeanour proper to a princess of Atiu and a great Belitani chieftain's daughter, the drawing out of the secret she wanted was as easy as spinning sinnet out of cocoanut husk.

Nothing is private in the Eastern Pacific, and it was not long before all the professor's personal affairs were tossing about like seaweed on the flood of general gossip—mostly unfit for publication—that surged about the apparently uninterested ears of the silent, splendid sea-queen throned on the pile of pandanus mats.... The Siamani (German) had got skulls in Niué, in Uea, in Mangaia, and was now collecting them about the Society group.... He was an ugly, grey-snouted pig to look at, and rooted in the earth like any pig; still, Taous and Mahina, daughters of Falani, seemed to think that—(details lost in a heated argument about the personal characteristics of the ladies).... Anyhow, Vekia from the hills said he was going to buy her two silk dresses from San Francisco when he came back from Falaite Island; so he was not as mean as he looked. Yes, he was going to Falaite Island in a great hurry; he would not even take time to finish his pig-rooting in Raiatea, on account of something he had heard from an old man who had once lived up in Falaite.... What fools the papalangi (whites) were. Did not every one in the Islands know about the old, old people that used to live on Falaite, hundreds of moons before the days of Tuti (Cook), and how they all died, and nobody lived there for very, very long, until some people wandered up from Niué in Tuti's time; and how the skulls of the old, old people were still there, buried in a cave that was a hundred miles long, and guarded by as many devils as would fill twenty war canoes? Of course, these things were known, and always had been—but when would any man of Tahiti or Raiatea have thought of such folly as travelling more than a thousand miles to fight the devils and take away the skulls? What if they were worth money enough to buy a big schooner, as the old grey pig had told Vekia when he promised her those dresses? Would a whole schooner, loaded down with dollars, be any good to a man after the devils had killed him? Vekia would never get her trade finery, for all her airs; and Jacky Te Vaka, whose schooner was to be hired to take the Siamani up to Falaite, would never come back from such a sacrilegious journey.... Why could he not wait, and go by Kapitani Satoni's schooner when she made her yearly trip by and by? Every one knew that the *Sipila* was under a charm, and no harm could come to any one on board her. But he would not wait, and just as soon as Jacky's boat came back from Bora-Bora, next week, they were to go.... Ahi! and Jacky was such a handsome man—it was a great pity!

Such was the substance of the information gathered by Vaiti. It resulted in her ordering the course of the ship to be changed, and heading direct for Friday Island, instead of going down to Auckland. Friday Island—out of the way, infertile, uninteresting, and little known—had been one of Saxon's private preserves for some years. He touched there once a year, purchased all the copra that the little place produced at his own price, and paid for it in cheap tinned meat, boxes of damaged biscuit, and tins of imitation salmon instead of cash. He seldom went ashore, and certainly did not waste his time cave-hunting, if he did chance to set foot on the beach. Vaiti, with her odd faculty for acquiring miscellaneous information, had known since the first time the *Sybil* called that there were great caves on the island, and that a devil of unusual quality and size guarded them. So much might have been said of a hundred similar islands, however, and she had not troubled herself about either caves or devils until the German professor's secret set her on the alert for something that looked like a dangerous, exciting, and profitable adventure.

# CHAPTER IV

## THE BLACK VIRI

Moreover, as Harris had said, she had been devoured with desire of a real Paris dress ever since her stay in the Wellington hotel. There had been a famous actress there at the same time, and all her garments had been freely paragraphed in the ladies' column of the local press. When she swam languidly through the hall of the Constantinople, shining mystic and wonderful out of a cloud of rainbow silks and chiffons that had cost a formidable row of figures in the Rue de la Paix, all the women caught their breath, looked once, and then gazed determinedly out of the windows, pretending that they had noticed nothing. When she came in to a late supper, floating in spangled mists and sparkling with constellations of diamonds, every head was turned her way, and half the heads—the short-cropped ones—stayed turned, in more senses than one. It was a revelation and a martyrdom to Vaiti. What were her muslin frocks and her ten new hats at a whole pound apiece compared to this? And the vision of money saved up faded away for the time being before the vision of one such frock—only one—belonging to her. Life could surely offer nothing more.

Of this, naturally, she said nothing to Pita, merely relating the matter of the skulls in as few words as possible. Pita, for his part, made no comment, but took a couple of revolvers out of the boat and thrust one into his belt, handing the other to the girl. Then he girded up his pareo—a significant action among islanders—and felt the handle of his knife to see that it was loose in the sheath. There was a large sack in the boat containing candles and food, and leaving ample space for other filling later on. Vaiti tossed it to Pita, and the two began their walk, barefoot, swift and silent, casting a quick glance every now and then among the weirdly stilted stems of the lonely pandanus groves as they went.

"They are all down with the *Sybil*—it is safer now than it would be at night," said Pita. "Vaiti, if we get these things, and sell them for much money in Sitani, you and I will leave the *Sybil* when she next goes to Atiu; and you shall be queen of Atiu and I shall be king, and we shall eat roast pork and 'uakari' every day."

"My father would burn the villages and kill the chiefs, and hang your head on the bowsprit of the ship," replied Vaiti conversationally. "Besides, I like Sitani, and I will buy myself a wonder dress from Palisi town there."

"Then we will leave at Sitani, and be great chiefs there, if these old bones indeed sell for so much money. And we will buy a little schooner for ourselves, and you shall be the real captain, and there will be four gold bands on your sleeve and one on the peak of your cap; and you shall get a *sitificati* from the chiefs of the great harbour, and take the schooner out of Sitani Heads yourself. And every one shall be afraid of me and you, and they will say——"

Vaiti had been listening as she swung along, now casting a glance of approval at the handsome lad while he spoke cunningly of the schooner she should command, now shooting out her lip a little, and slashing impatiently with her knife at the young cocoanut fronds. Suddenly, looking very straight ahead, she interrupted.

"Pita, you talk too fast. There are things you do not know. Tell me, is your heart strong within you?"

"It is strong," answered the island Maori.

"Then listen. There is a devil in the cave."

"I do not believe in devils. I am misinari, and go to church five times on Sundays; also I have a black coat and two boots very nearly the same as each other to wear on collection days."

"There is a devil all the same; you do not know everything that is in the world, little Pita," replied Vaiti. "There is something bad there. I do not believe in native devils, for I am 'papa-langi'; but I know there is—a thing of some kind—there. A bad thing. A black viri, they say, but I do not understand that."

"A black viri is nothing. You and I do not mind such things. See—there will perhaps be one in this rotten wood." Pita struck and kicked at a mass of decaying cocoanut wood, and hunted out one of the great black centipedes that are common in the equatorial islands.

There is nothing on the bosom of Mother Earth more loathly than the centipede, and Pita's quarry—nearly a foot long, as thick as a sausage, scarlet feelers on its hideous head, and scarlet legs fringing its long lithe body—was as hideous a specimen as ever jerked itself lightning-wise across a forest path. Pita, however, with swift dexterity, seized the horrible beast by the neck and tail, holding it so that it could neither bite nor sting, and lifted it up to his companion. Vaiti's eyes dilated ever so little. She drew her knife and slashed the creature in two; then, stooping down, she struck at the flying halves as they ran away in opposite directions, and cut them up into mincemeat. Leaving the red fragments still wriggling in the track amidst an unsavoury, snaky smell, she stepped swiftly on.

"It is no matter," she said. "We two shall see what we shall see. Keep your heart warm within you."

"And if we come back safe?" cried the impetuous Pita, catching the girl's warm round arms in his two sinewy hands, and letting his black eyes gaze into hers.

Vaiti stood very still for a moment, looking out to sea. The spell of her stillness fell on Pita, and he remained as if frozen. Far away the surf hummed on the reef, and a sea-bird cried. Above the two beautiful, motionless young figures the palms rustled endlessly in the long trade wind.

"... If we come back" ... said Vaiti at last, her eyes still fixed on the far-off line of the outer sea—"if we come back—we will go away together, you and I."

She looked so like a witch in a trance (such things are not unknown even now, in strange Atiu) that Pita's hands dropped from her arms, and he felt half frightened in the moment of his triumph. But Vaiti recalled him to himself by starting her steady swing again, and saying with a laugh, as they footed it through the dry, sun-struck woods side by side:

"I think some day my father will make a parrot cage to hang a green Atiu parrot in, and it will be made of your ribs and breast-bone, little Pita—all the same as my grandfather did in the islands to the man who stole his wife."

At that moment the woods opened out and the cave came into view—a velvet-dark blot in the dazzling glare of greenery that tangled itself about the shoreward cliffs.

Pita's hand sprang to his revolver, and he uttered an exclamation of angry surprise. Beside the cave stood a tall, brown, naked figure painted like a witch-doctor and armed with a spear.

"Do not shoot," said Vaiti quickly. "It will do no good. Let me look to him myself."

She walked right up to the native, stood within a yard of him, and stared at him, in a silence that somehow managed to express unflattering things. The man, stamping the butt of his spear on the ground, turned away from her and addressed Pita.

"I have nothing to do with this woman of yours," he said. "It is with men I would speak."

"Speak, then, pig-face," said Pita insolently, hoping to provoke a fight, since the man seemed to be alone.

"Enter if you wish," replied the other. "We have sent no fighting-men to hinder you; the way is clear. Yet if you think the hot sun on the pleasant land is good to see, and the beating of the warm heart in the living breast is sweet to feel, go not into our sacred caves, to lay evil hands upon the holy bones of Falaiti. Enough."

The man's words were strangely void of heat or anger, and he held his spear loosely, Vaiti did not suspect an ambush, for she knew that no native would enter the cave. Yet in that moment her quick mind leaped to the knowledge of some unknown danger threatening herself and Pita from out the cold-breathing world of darkness that lay within that rugged arch, and for one prophetic instant she could smell the very smell of death.

But Vaiti's courage was of the kind that rises, wave by wave, the higher for all obstacle, and her spirit swelled within her to flood-tide in that moment. She turned upon the witch-doctor and laughed in his face. Then she stretched out her hand, and Pita's leaped into it, warm and strong, and together they stepped over the threshold of the cave.

The man outside cursed them, slowly and with relish.

"Shall we not kill him?" asked Pita.

"There is no use," said Vaiti. "It is plain to me that all the tribe know, and they trust to the dangers of the place, whatever these may be. This island is at the very end of the world, it is true, and strange things may happen here."

"Yes, there is nothing that one might not believe in this place," said Pita, looking back. Already the gloom of Hades itself was winding about them, and the air struck gravelike and cold. In the distance the mouth of the cave cast a brief glow of emerald light upon the dewy ferns and mosses close to the threshold, so that they shone like the jewelled foliage of some magic forest in a fairy play. Then came the dripping roof, the enormous stalactite buttresses of the cave, dimly edged with light; the oozing floor, and the lifeless dark.

Vaiti spoke not at all, as they walked side by side down dark tunnel after dark tunnel, across empty, thunderous-echoing black halls and archways—their little candles flitting like fireflies through a dim world of unconquerable gloom. Pita, however, was strangely gay. He yelled aloud to set the echoes booming in the black domes above, when they crossed some invisible great goblin market-place, full of hollow sounds and half-glimpsed monstrosities. He sang when the way along the endless corridors grew tedious, and the glistening stalactite candelabra succeeded one another, thick as forest branches, for mile after mile unchanged. When the path was barred by inky lakes of unknown depth and ghastly chill, and the two explorers had to tie their lights on their heads and swim for it, he pretended to cry at the cold, and played tricks on Vaiti by slipping behind her and catching her feet in his teeth. So they went on, one in wild spirits, the other silent and grave. And the hours of the sunny day slipped by dark and changeless, as they passed farther and farther away life and light into the cold black depths of the cave.

When it was about noon, as near as they could guess, Vaiti took the biscuits and tinned meat out of the sack, and they ate, squatting on the wet floor of the tunnel. They knew that the journey was a long one, and that the way could not well be missed, yet they were beginning to feel a little uneasy now. Did this cave go on for ever?

Somehow, the food did not cheer them and when they rose and went on again they did not talk. And now a worse difficulty than any they had yet encountered suddenly barred the way. The winding tunnel along which they were walking turned sharp round a corner, and then ended to all appearance in nothing. They stood at the edge of an empty gulf, black as a starless sky and of depth unknowable. Thin trickles of light, from the candles wavered faintly about its edges, and showed that the colossal crack had a farther side, but it was impossible to see what lay beyond, and the depth below cast back the candle rays as an armoured hull throws off a rifle bullet.

Pita detached a lump of rock and threw it over the edge. Vaiti watched him with sombre eyes. "There is no bottom there," she said. "It goes through the earth, and out on the other side; that is what I think."

"Children's talk," said Pita, listening intently. There was an echoing rattle as the stone bounded from side to side on its way down. The rattle grew fainter and fainter, diminished to a sound like the ticking of a watch, faded to an almost imperceptible vibration, and then seemed to die out. Seemed—for although there was nothing left for the ear to catch, the sharpened sensory nerves of the body still responded to a faint tingle, somewhere, somehow, long after the actual sound had faded away.

"I told you," said Vaiti. "There is no bottom." Pita did not answer; he was measuring the narrowest part of the gulf with his eye, and estimating the value of the three short steps of a run that were possible before taking off.

"It is not two fathoms wide here," he said, throwing the provision sack across to judge his distance better in the uncertain light. Yet, despite the three steps of a run, there was not an inch to spare when he landed on the other side, with an effort that strained every muscle of his powerful young body.

"Can you jump it?" he called to Vaiti—without any particular anxiety, for the Maori has no nerves, and he knew what the girl could do aloft on the schooner.

To his astonishment, Vaiti made no answer, but stood leaning up against the wall of the tunnel, both hands pressed against her chest. In a moment more she was violently sick.

"The smell!" she said presently, turning a ghastly face towards the light of Pita's candle.

"I smell nothing," said Pita, puzzled. "The wind blows your way. There is perhaps some dead thing down there."

Vaiti shook her head, and Pita saw that her eyes seemed to fill half her face as she looked down into the gulf. Suddenly she sprang, her white drapery flying behind her, and landed half a yard behind Pita, with a leap that drew a cry of wonder from the Atiuan. "Come, come," she said, taking his hand and fairly dragging him on.

They had little farther to go. The tunnel wound on for perhaps another hundred yards, and then stopped. They found themselves in a low-roofed circular chamber, such as is often met with at the end of long underground passages—a small, insignificant place, roofed with drooping green stalactites and floored with shapeless, slimy hummocks of stalagmite. Numbers of deep shelves were quarried out in the rocky sides, and in these lay, row on row, the bare, mouldering skulls of Falaite's long-ago chiefs—many of them cracked and split, and not a few fallen into shapeless fragments, though there were a score or two in excellent condition. They were curious skulls indeed, had their discoverers been able to understand them. In the projecting jaws, huge canines, strangely high cranium, and oddly developed ridges near the opening of the ear were the materials of a problem contradictory and complicated enough to occupy the wits of a whole college of science. But Vaiti and Pita saw none of these things. They only noted with disappointment, that most of the skulls had gone to decay—picked out the best of the unbroken specimens, packed the great sack full of them, and turned homewards.

"Vaiti," said Pita, as they walked down the rocky tunnel, and felt the slope of the gulf beginning under their feet. "Vaiti, what did you——"

Her face, turned back upon him, slew the still-born question on his lips.

It was scarce a minute before the chasm gaped in their path yet again. The leap was worse on this side, for the clustered cones of stalagmite did not allow a fair take-off. Pita looked calculatingly at the farther side, very dimly visible in the faint candle-light, and picked up a fallen stalactite to throw across.

"Do not throw!" said Vaiti, in a breathless whisper.

"Why not? I can jump better if I hear where it hits," replied Pita, casting the stone before Vaiti had time to snatch at his hand. It fell short, and rolled down into the chasm with a loud, crashing noise.

"Fool! fool! Jump quickly!" exclaimed Vaiti, in the same strained, horrible whisper.... Just for a second before he sprang, Pita looked down into the black pit beneath, and it seemed to him that the darkness shirred and shivered below the farther edge of the crevasse—that for the fragment of a second something long, red, whiplike, vibrated high up in the light of the candles, and then was gone.... There was a sickening odour in the air—a living smell, not a dead one; there was a sliding, rustling sound....

"Jump!" shrieked Vaiti.

They leaped through the air as one, but it was only Vaiti who landed on the farther side. Behind her, as she touched the rock, rose a shriek that blasted the leaden air into red-hot drops of horror—that went on and on and on, tearing upwards to the vaulted roof like a rocket fired from the mouth of hell; breaking at last into a gasping bellow, and snapping off into grisly silence on the very crest of a long, choking roar, in which there was nothing left of human.

... Pita had jumped short. Falling on the far side, with his legs half over the abyss, he had grasped for an instant at Vaiti's outstretched hands, and in the very act had been snatched away—snatched by a long, ghastly head, armed with poisoned jaws and quivering red antennas, that shot with the speed of a bullet out from the depths of the chasm, and back again with its prey.... The head was a foot long at least, the horrible winnowing feelers more than a yard, the black and red body, that just flashed into view for a second, was as thick as a man's thigh. It was a nightmare, an impossibility, and yet ... it was, beyond doubt, the Black Viri.

For a little while it seemed to Vaiti that she went mad, and then that the world went out and she died. A long time after, she found herself sitting on the floor of the tunnel, her head badly bruised and cut where she had dashed it against the rock, her candle guttering down towards extinction, her revolver empty and smelling of powder—she did not remember in the least how it had become so—and the whole black, horrible place still and silent as the bottom of the sea. Pita was gone. The bag of skulls had disappeared—fallen, no doubt, into the abyss. There was not a movement or a sound, save the whisper of the water—drops trickling ceaselessly from the roof into the dark pools upon the ground.

\* \* \* \* \*

That evening, when the early starlight was beginning to shine down upon the creepers veiling the mouth of the tunnel, Saxon, sober at last, and rushing like a madman to the cave to find his daughter, met Vaiti herself coming down the rocks at the entrance, haggard, trembling, and almost old. He asked for Pita, and was answered only by a shuddering gesture of the hands.

Questioning no more, he carried the girl down to the beach and brought her on board the schooner. There, when they had sailed, he left her undisturbed in her cabin for many days, while they ran steadily southward to pleasant Auckland and the temperate latitudes, farther and farther away from lonely, sun-smitten Falaite. The story of the day in the cave was known to him, as to every one on the island, for the witch-doctor of Falaite had told it far and wide, reserving only the one interesting fact—how he became possessed of the information. And as no one else alive on Falaite knew that there were two ways of reaching the skull-chamber, and more than one place where a man could hide unseen, the witch-doctor's reputation as a prophet and a clairvoyant was greatly increased; so that he suffered continually from a happily-acquired indigestion, and his dogs grew fat on bones of pig and fowl. And no one came ever any more into the sacred caves of Falaite Island.

Saxon declared plumply that he did not believe the tale, opining rather that the "blanked old wizard Johnnie had shoved Pita into the hole himself, and good riddance of bad rubbish, too."

None the less, he was uneasy at Vaiti's rather prolonged depression, and though he dared not break in upon her solitude further than to hand her in her meals and ask her how she felt, now and then, he listened almost constantly at her state-room door, and gave up whisky for at least ten days.

About the eleventh day, Te Ai, a young Samoan A.B., sat upon the main hatch in the pleasant coolness of the second dog-watch, and sang the farewell song of sweet Samoa, "Good-bye, my F'lennie"—the song that plucks so surely at the heartstrings of all who have ever loved and sailed away among the far-off fairy islands of the wide South Seas.


"Good-bye, my F'lennie (friend)—o le a o tea,

Efau lau le va'a, o le alii pule i...."


he sang, beating time with his knees on the hatch.... Then suddenly he stopped, and the little group of mates and captain on the poop did not see why.

Later on, Harris, his face stiff with suppressed laughter, knocked at the captain's door.

"Can you oblige me with a piece of sticking-plaster, sir?" he said.

"Who for?" asked Saxon, reaching for the yellow roll that lies handy in every shipmaster's cabin about the peaceful Pacific.

"Te Ai, sir. He's been knocked down, and his head got cut against the pump."

"Who did it?" bristled Saxon, ready to uphold his own peculiar privileges, at once.

"She did, sir," said Harris, nearly choking. "Te Ai, he was singin' 'Good-bye, my F'lennie,' on the main 'atch and out she come from the deck cabin like a—like a nurricane, begging your pardon, sir—and she ups with a belayin' pin from the rail, an——"

"All right, all right; there's your plaster," interrupted Saxon. "Harris! Here."

"Yes, sir!"

"Give this to Te Ai."

"Lor' bless you, sir, 'e don't mind; 'e's a——"

"You do what you're told. Stop. Where's my daughter?"

"Walkin' on the poop, sir, uncommon lively, and looking like dirty weather ahead."

"That's all right," sighed the captain, with an air of infinite relief.

# CHAPTER V

## A DIAMOND WEB

It was six o'clock in Apia, and the round sun was hanging low above the rim of the level sea, like a burning coal ready to drop down upon a breadth of hyacinth silk. The stores were closed along the straggling beach street, where the sand was white under foot, and parrakeets tweedled cheerily in the scarlet-flowered flamboyant trees. Native dandies, greatly oiled and dyed, and wearing a bright hibiscus blossom over each ear, swung past with the inimitable Samoan roll, their golden brown limbs gay with the red-and-white English bath-towel that is popular as full dress for steamer days in the little island capital. Girls with high-coiffed yellow heads and pink or green tunics wandered lazily home to the cool, dark-domed native houses open all round to the sunset sky. They went in groups, and sang as they walked—windy, fitful gusts of strange island melody, breaking out and dying away like the evening breeze among the heavy-headed palms. Smells of yam and breadfruit, brown from the baking pits, of fish cooked in green, savoury leaves, and taro spinach stewed with cocoanut cream, crept out upon the cooling air. The long, hot day was done, and Apia rested and ate.

In "Charley's"—the least reputable of Apia's tavern-hotels—the egregious *table d'hôte* was in full progress out in the green-shuttered verandah. Charley himself, an oily, flashy New Caledonian half-caste, dressed in striped pyjamas, was eating curried tin—nature unknown—with a knife and two fingers, at the head of the table. A corpse-faced Chinese was shuffling round with the inevitable Pacific fowl, cut up in a watery soup. The table-cloth was of linoleum, the swinging lamp guttered and smoked, the cutlery was dislocated and black. But there was English beer on the bar counter, and plenty of broken ice; and the whisky that mounted high in each man's smeary tumbler was good of its kind. Charley knew his customers, and sought first the essential.

Captain Saxon, his schooner safe at anchor outside, and his copra advantageously sold to an Auckland agent, sat eating at the table, heavy-faced, a little intoxicated, and almost absolutely blank in mind. This was his nearest approach to happiness, and one that he enjoyed often enough, for, since thought meant pain to him, he had managed to acquire a wonderful agility in avoiding it, and to live for the most part almost as purely by instinct and impulse as a dog.

It was perhaps for this reason that he did not notice anything unusual in the demeanour of that singularly unknown quantity, Vaiti, his daughter. And yet Vaiti—sombre and sparkling in a dress of vaporous red, with a handful of star stephanotis from the verandah thrust into the marvellous waves of her hair—was evidently not quite herself. She sat a little apart from the noisy company that sprawled about the table, looked at no one, ate her food absent-mindedly and pulled little strips off the decaying oilcloth of the table-cover with a steady industry that made Charley wriggle in his seat, although he did not dare to remonstrate.

Some one else was watching her, if Saxon was not. A short, stocky man, with burning grey eyes, a fiery red beard, and a sharp furrow between the eyebrows, that somehow suggested belaying-pins and rope's ends, was looking at her every now and then as he noisily sucked in his soup. The inspection did not appear to please him altogether. He finished his dinner quickly, took the current glass of whisky in his hand, and rolled off to the dark end of the verandah, followed by a grey-haired, greasy-faced mate who had been sitting beside him.

"Still on for it, cap?" asked the latter, leaning over the railing with an air of careless ease that contrasted oddly with his watchful eye.

"Yes, blank asterisk your condemned foolishness, sure I am on for it!" replied the captain, betraying his nationality by a slight touch of brogue.

There is no nation that swings so high and so low between opposite extremes of character as the impetuous race that is handcuffed, by an odd freak of geography, to steady, serious England. Great saints and great rogues are commoner in Ireland than ordinary people, and each displays the fullest flavour of his kind. Donahue, master of the island schooner *Ikurangi*, was, or had been, Irish; and it was assuredly not the company of the saints that claimed his membership.

The two spoke together for a little while in level tones that sounded loud and careless enough, yet somehow did not carry. One learns these things by practice.

"She smells a rat, I'm thinking," said the old mate, looking critically the while at Charley, as if he were valuing the half-caste's clothes for pawn.

"Let her. You and I are apt to be a match for her, for all that," answered the captain. He looked at Charley also. You would have sworn the two were discussing him, and rather unfavourably. Charley himself shifted in his seat, and showed his magnificent teeth uncomfortably.

"Think she'll come on board?"

Vaiti was watching them, her chin on her hand. Her expression was not to be read.

"I'll get her on board all right," answered the captain, keeping his eyes away from the girl with an effort. "You play up, that's all."

"'Jer think you're a match for that weasel in a woman's skin—you or any of us?"

"I do, then. Forty's a match for twenty any day in the year, if the heads of them comes anything near equal. Cunnin' as Old Nick she is, but I've been cunnin' twenty years longer than her."

"You pitched her a good yarn, I'll lay."

"I did that—about the derelick we boarded nor'-east of the Paumotus, and the Spanish ladies' clothes and cases of goods that was lying about, and how we took what there was, includin' of a di'mond necklashe that was sittin' all its lone on the table in the old man's cabin (Be minding me, now, or you'll be making mistakes), and the way a gale riz on us before we was through, and hurried us back to the *Ikurangi*, so that we lost the derelick, and didn't see no more of her; and how we heard in Noumea afterwards that there was like to be joolery on boord her, so that we're all on to go and find her again."

"Straight fact up to finding the di'monds, and gory lyin' after that, I see. But how d'ye make out the people that deserted the ship was such fat-headed idiots as to leave the joolery?"

"Why, they was fat-headed idiots right enough; they did leave a good lot of saleable stuff, as you and I knows; and it's only addin' on a bit to say that the ship had been on fire and made them clear for their lives, so that they didn't think of the valuables. There's the necklashe I have for proof. And, mind me now, what we heard was that the people of the ship knows now that she didn't go down, and will be out after her themselves when they can raise the cash, so that hurry's the word."

"How much of that's true?"

"Not a —— bit. The people was drowned, I allow. But it hangs well, and don't you go and forget none of it. I pitched the yarn that way because of that bit of pashtry joolery I got hould of in mistake for goods down Melbourne way.... I misremember if I tould you."

"You did, more nor once, and you was jolly well served right by her," candidly replied the mate. "The yarn's all right, I suppose, and the paste necklace is good business; but where does this Vaiti come in?"

"Quit lookin' at her, ye —— fool, and give me a light for me poipe. Talk easy, can't you.... Why, she knows more navigation than most men that's got a master's ticket, and she's as vain of it as a paycock. And that's how I'll have her. Always get a woman t'rough her consate, me boy, especially if her eyes are too sharp in common. That'll pull the wool over them when nothing else will."

"When I was in Callao——" began the mate, with an evil chuckle.

"Leave Callao be now; you can tell me about her another time. Well, you understand about Saxon's girl, I hope? She's to navigate us on the trip, because nayther you nor I knows enough for a cruisin' job like this, and the old chap himself is pretty general drunk—that's the way I put it—and shares with what we find, and the ould divil himself to come along, just for propriety, and in case of a fight with the owners. Oh, a nate yarn, and she shwallowed it down like a cat atin' butter. She's comin' on boord to-night, to see the necklashe and look over the chart I've marked. She'll not bring ould Saxon, for she's feared of nayther man nor divil, and I'll bet she thinks to get the bearin's of the place off of me and chate me out of it after all."

"And how the h—— do you think she's going to believe that you give the show away before the ship sails? Her teeth wasn't cut yesterday, by all we know."

"Faith, and we do know!" muttered the captain, with a horrible undercurrent of oaths. "And she'll know, by —— she will! I'd slit the throat of her, if it wasn't for the other bit of divarsion we've planned."

"Say you've planned," interrupted the mate darkly. "I call it bad work, whether she was man, woman, or child; but you're my master."

"And you're a plashter saint, ain't you?" sneered the captain. "Let's have no more of your chat; we know each other a —— sight too well. As for the chart, she'll think we don't mean to give it away till she and her father is under sail with us, but she'll come on the chance of sneaking it out somehow. And when we've got her aboard, why—lave it to me! Ould Saxon's hell-cat daughter won't take no more pearl-shell beds from us or any one else."

"You ain't afraid of her knowing who we are?"

"How would she, then? The *Ikurangi* isn't the *Margaret Macintyre*—bad luck to her who brought me down to such a tub, after ownin' the finest auxiliary in Auckland!—and she never seen you or me till to-day. No, it's all right. That's enough jaw; you go aboard, and attend to you know what, and then send off the boat for her and me."

Vaiti, curly classic head on slender hand, still watched from her corner.

Did she suspect? There was nothing for suspicion to lay hold of. Donahue was one of the acutest villains under the Southern Cross, and he did not make clumsy mistakes. The story of the derelict, of the valuables abandoned on board, of the necessity for finding the ship soon and secretly, might have sounded far-fetched to city-dwelling folk, but out in the wild South Seas stranger things may happen any day. The plan was neat and plausible from every point of view, and Vaiti had taken the bait readily enough that afternoon. Yet Donahue felt—as the two walked silently down the dim, perfumed beach street, all ablow with vagrant sea winds and wandering wafts of song—that he would have given a good deal for just one peep into his handsome companion's mind.

Vaiti walked beside him, looking straight ahead. Had Donahue's wish been granted, he would have thought somewhat less of his own acuteness. She did suspect. A man, in her case, would have been convinced by the reasonable aspect of the whole affair. Vaiti, being a woman, with sea-anemone tentacles of instinct floating and tingling all about the steady centres of reason in her mind, was convinced, and yet not convinced. She thought it was all right, yet she knew it was not—after a woman's way.

In any case, however, it was an adventure, and there was a mystery to fathom. So she put on a more substantial dress than the gauzy draperies she had been wearing, hung the neatest possible little pearl-handled Smith and Wesson round her neck, under the swelling folds of her frock, by means of an innocent-looking thin gold neck-chain that would snap with a tug; put her long-bladed knife in her pocket, with the sheath sewn to the dress, so that a pull would bring out the blade, and joined Donahue an hour after dinner, on the verandah steps, confident of her ability to see the thing through, whatever it might be.

She looked sharply about her, as she stepped over the low bulwarks of the *Ikurangi* and dropped down on to the encumbered, untidy deck. No one about. Nothing to be seen but a dirty little main deck, with rusty pumps and a yawning hatch, and a poop that even in the pallid light just beginning to tremble up from the rising moon showed neglect of the sacred ceremony of daily deck-washing.

Now, any decent ship's captain will attend to his deck-washing, even if he doesn't shave or wash himself from port to port. Vaiti did not like that unscrupulous, dirty poop. But she was already up on it, and Donahue was bowing her down the cabin companion, with a jarring smile and a good deal of over-fluent blarney. The cabin was small and smelly; it had an oblong table in the middle, surrounded by cushioned lockers, and an open door at the end facing the companion. This door evidently opened into Donahue's own cabin, for a rough wash-stand and a looking-glass, the latter hung high on the bulkhead, were plainly visible. There was a lamp nailed above the glass, and the two together shone brightly out into the rather ill-lit main cabin.

"What'll you take?" asked Donahue, with his unpleasant smile. "I've got some sweet sherry wine, just the thing for ladies—or wouldn't ye put your lips to a taste of peach brandy?"

Vaiti shook her head.

"No good drink, suppose talk business," she said. She would not have swallowed a glass of water on the *Ikurangi* for a dozen Virot hats.

Donahue had not expected to catch her so easily; still, he cast a thought of regret to his nicely-doctored liquors. She evidently meant what she said— and the other way Was harder.

"Well, thin, darlin', we'll have a look at the cha-art," he observed, producing a roll of paper. "It's yourself that can help us t'rough this business—you and the ould man—better than any one from Calloa to Sydney if only yez are raisonable about terms."

He spread the chart out on the table, and weighted it down with a couple of tumblers.

Vaiti, her mind charged full with watchful suspicion, felt that sudden small, sick thrill that is the forerunner of the thought—"I wish I hadn't!" Afterwards, when she came to think matters over, she knew that it was because Donahue had made the mistake of bringing out the chart before the terms had been discussed, which was an improbable sort of thing to do. In such moments, however, one does not think, one only feels. Still, the warning was unmistakable, and Vaiti made as if to rise, intending to plead sudden illness and get out on deck. But Donahue, sharp as a snake, saw the movement, and brought out his trump card at once.

"Sure, I'm a —— fool, I am, to forget the necklashe! You haven't seen that yet," he said, whipping a stream of white fire out of his pocket and letting it fall across the dark wood of the table. It was a magnificent piece of paste-work, and had taken in Donahue himself, some few weeks ago, after a fashion that made him sore enough to remember. Vaiti gasped when she saw it, and laid both her pretty olive hands upon it at once. Her suspicions were not exactly killed, but they had for the moment no room to live with the passionate feeling aroused by the gems. Donahue, with his unspeakable experience of the sex, had calculated rightly when he classified her among the women who would almost do murder for a diamond.... Such jewels! and she had never had one in her hand before, though her eyes had often filled and her heart ached with hopeless desire before the maddening glories of the jewellers' windows in Auckland and Sydney.

She hugged the necklace to her breast like a baby, she shook it, she danced it in the light.... And then, was it in woman's nature to refrain from snapping the clasp about her neck, and feeling the dear touch of those cold drops and pendants on her bosom?

"Ah, now, but you're the beauty wit' them little jokers round your neck! And the lovely neck you have, darlin'!" blarneyed Donahue. He had better have been silent, for Vaiti, used to admiration of every kind and degree as to daily bread, felt the falseness of the tone. If all other men admired her beauty, this one did not, though he said so. His grey, goat-like eyes looked something more like hate across the narrow table, under the ill-smelling oily lamp, and Vaiti saw they did.

Donahue, taught by twenty years of active villainy, was quick to feel the necessity for the next move. He went into his own cabin and turned up the lamp. The looking-glass shone out brightly under its rays.

"Come and look at yourself, me beauty," he said; "and let me ould shavin'-glass see the handsomest girl in the islands wearin' what she ought to wear every day of her life, if she'd her rights."

For the moment, Vaiti was not herself. She was drunk with the jewels; she was crazed with the desire to see herself in them. If heaven and hell had stood between her and the looking-glass, she was bound to go to it, and Donahue knew it, as surely as he knew that the moon would set that night.

Vaiti—still sensing the danger that she would not heed, through all the intoxication of the jewels—thought, in a cinematographic flash, that one was safe before a glass, at all events.... No one could come up behind you.... Besides, there was the little revolver, hanging on the chain that would snap with a tug....

And then, for the space of a full minute, she saw nothing, knew nothing, lived for nothing but the sight of her own dark, beautiful face in the glass, lit up into surpassing loveliness by the scintillating fires about her neck. There was no movement in the mirror behind her. Donahue sat motionless at the table, and the cabin was very still.

... The first ecstasy subsided, and she turned her head a little to see the diamonds twinkle....

Donahue's elbow knocked a glass off the table with a sharp crash. Almost at the same instant two powerful hands closed on each of Vaiti's ankles, and snatched her feet from under her. She plucked out the revolver as she fell, but her hands were caught, whisked behind her, and securely tied, with a prompt swiftness that told of frequent experience. In another minute her ankles were lashed together, none too gently; she was carried into a small state-room, thrown down upon the bunk, and left alone in the dark, with the slam of the door and snap of the lock resounding in her ears.

Most women would have screamed. Vaiti remembered that they were out in the middle of a wide harbour, and decided not to risk the infliction of a gag for such a slight chance of rescue.... Certain ugly scenes on the *Sybil* rose up before her eyes. No; decidedly it was her only policy to keep quiet.

Outside there was the thud of bare feet running about the deck, the creak of the booms rising on the masts, the slatting of loose sails—loud orders, long yells from the native crew, as they pulled and hauled. The *Ikurangi* was making sail.

Then sudden silence, slow heeling over of the cabin, lip-lap of hurrying water along the hull. They were off. Where? God—or the devil—only knew!

# CHAPTER VI

## MAROONED

There was plenty of time for reflection in the long days that followed. The greasy-faced old mate came in and cut the lashings off Vaiti's ankles and wrists, a few hours after sailing, and she was left free to move about the cabin, which offered a promenade of exactly seven feet by three. Meals were handed in to her three times daily—the usual black tea, tinned meat, and weevily biscuit of second-class island schooners—and she was not in any way molested, though the door was always kept locked. Donahue put in his head once or twice to look at her, as she sat cross-legged on her bunk, staring out through the port at the tumbling seas. He generally had something to say— a jarring, mocking compliment, or a remark about the time they were likely to make Sydney Heads—knowing all the time that Vaiti could estimate the general direction of their course by the sun, and that there was no southing in it. If she had ever feared any one, she feared this man—almost.

It was not difficult to understand how the capture had been brought about. A man under the bunk, another under the sofa opposite—her own eyes watching only the upper part of the cabin as reflected in the glass—nothing could be simpler or better planned. The affair was none the less ugly on that account. Perhaps it was only Vaiti's burning anger at her utter rout and defeat in her own business of plotting and intrigue that saved her from something very like despair, as the schooner ploughed steadily on, day after day, carrying her into the great unknown, farther and farther away from all who could defend her. Yet, despairing or not, Saxon's daughter never lost her courage. They had taken her weapons from her as they carried her into the cabin, but they could not take away her undaunted spirit. She waited her time.

As to the meaning of the business, she trusted, again, to time's enlightenment. Saxon had many enemies; so had she. It would all come out by-and-by. Meantime, it was clear that no one meant to murder her. What else might be meant she could not tell, and she did not care to speculate overmuch. Under such circumstances one does best to save one's nerve against the time it may be wanted.

It was on the twenty-third day out from Apia, bearing, as far as she could discover, in a north-westerly direction, that she first noted the approach of land. Nothing could be seen from her side of the ship, but she heard the long, excited cries of the island crew, and the thundering of their feet, as they began putting the ship about with unwonted vigour, to a chorus of native songs. She strained her eyes eagerly when the ship came about on the other tack, but the line of the horizon was unbroken; and it was not for another hour that she saw, from her low elevation, what the look-out in the crow's nest had sighted long before—a line of small black bristles pricking the edge of the horizon several miles away.

Vaiti knew the sight at once for the palms of a low atoll island—evidently some barren, sun-smitten spot close up to the line—and a ready solution of the whole puzzling affair at once sprang into her mind.

Marooning!

Most people know the meaning of this term; nearly every one has heard of sailors captured by pirates in old days, and left on lonely islands, or even deserted by their own comrades on some isolated spot, with just enough food and water to save the marooners' consciences from the guilt of actual murder. Vaiti knew both the word and the thing very well-indeed, and she was almost certain that the *Ikurangi* had gone off the course on the way to some South American port with the view of hiding her where she would not easily be found again. There are many islands in the wastes of the vast Pacific where a ship may not pass once in half a century, and these—unlike the typical "desert" island of stories—are almost always barren, hungry, shadeless spots, where Crusoe himself would have been hard put to it to make a decent living. The fertile, mountainous, well-watered isle is never without a native population, permanent or occasional, and is very seldom indeed, in these days, without a trader as well, and a regularly calling schooner. As for the breadfruit, oranges, pineapples, the pigs and goats, the sugarcane and maize of uninhabited islands as known to fiction, they have no counterpart in real life. All the valuable food plants and all useful animals are the product of importation and cultivation, ancient or modern. It follows, that where there are no people and no ships, there is nothing worth having.

Vaiti knew this very well, and decided that if she was going to be marooned, she might as well make such provision as circumstances allowed. She had hunted over every inch of the cabin—which seemed to belong to the mate—during the long days of the voyage, and she knew exactly what it contained. From the stores put away under the bunk she selected a large new sheet, which she concealed under her dress; a small stock of needles and thread, a box or two of matches, some hooks and line, and a stick of dynamite, evidently meant for some forgotten fishing purpose. There was nothing in the shape of a knife, much to her regret; and there was a good deal of clothing that she would have liked to carry away; but it would not do to take more than she could easily conceal. So she made an end of her preparations, and sat down to wait once more.

There was no moon that night until very late, and darkness came down so close on the stroke of four bells that Vaiti felt sure they were very near the equator. No one came near her, and tea seemed to be unusually late. The anchor-chain roared home soon after dark, the ship lay very still, and there was a good deal of running about on deck. Vaiti was confirmed in her anticipations of an uninhabited island by the fact that no boat was to be heard coming off from shore. Not a sound of any kind, indeed, came from the island, and there were no lights on the beach. Some one handed her in her tea by-and-by, and a little later her door was flung open again by the mate.

"Come on out," he said.

Vaiti followed the mate out of the cabin at once, rather to his surprise. She had made up her mind that anything was better than the *Ikurangi*, and she was looking out sharply for a chance—any chance—of turning the tables.

It did not look at first as if she were to have one. The dinghy had been swung out when she got on deck, and a couple of men were standing ready to lower away. They were islanders, and she knew that they would befriend her if they could—indeed, their glances showed as much—yet what could they do?

Donahue was nowhere visible. He had planned this business with some forethought, and he wanted to have a chance of casting blame on his subordinate if any inquisitive Government official should incline to look the matter up later on. So he stayed down in his own cabin, pretending to be asleep, and the mate, rather against his will, had to carry out orders alone.

Just as the boat was ready to lower away, one of the men let her go with a run, and she struck the water stern first, with a terrible splash. The mate, screaming curses, ran over to the falls and began to abuse the crew. The dinghy was injured, and they had to haul her up and swing out the whaleboat instead.

This took some little time, and Vaiti was forgotten for the moment—a chance that made her heart beat with eagerness to profit by it.

Two ideas held possession of her—that she must plan to secure a boat, and that she must manage to do the *Ikurangi* some sort of mischief. Was it to be borne that Donahue should go unpaid? The blood of a hundred fierce Island chiefs made answer.

Concerning the boat, she thought she saw a chance. They were bound to stay a day for wood and water, and that should furnish an opportunity. But the other matter?

If she could only get hold of the ship's papers and destroy them! That would be satisfactory. She knew, none better, that a ship's papers are her character, her "marriage-lines" of respectability. Without them a vessel is an illegitimate, furtive creature, every man's hand against her, every official eye turned coldly upon her. Vaiti would have liked very well to get hold of the *Ikurangi's*.

But, careless as Donahue was, the papers were not to be found in the little deck cabin which he used as a chart-room. Vaiti, disappointed, took one of the charts and began studying the position of the ship, with a view to finding out the name of the island off which they were lying. The chart was almost a blank, nothing being marked upon its wide expanse but a number of reefs and two or three atolls—Bilboa Island, Vaka, Ngamaru—dotted hundreds of miles apart in a naked waste of white. Bilboa, an abandoned guano island, of which she had heard something, seemed to Vaiti the most likely of the three spots. Ngamaru, she knew, had a native population, and about Vaka she could for the moment remember nothing, although she knew she had heard something once upon a time. All this part of the Pacific was far removed from the *Sybil's* haunts, and indeed from the haunts of any other ship of which Vaiti had ever heard.

It did not seem to be a healthy place for schooners; the reefs round both Vaka and Bilboa were many, and most were marked "Position doubtful." Donahue was evidently not familiar with either place, for the chart was freshly pencilled over with notes and corrections. Vaiti's heart leaped up as she looked at the careless work.... She saw a way.

They were still clearing the lumber out of the whaleboat on deck. No one was watching.

Vaiti took a pencil and rubber, and began to do some artistic alterations on the chart, helped by her knowledge of seamanship. In ten minutes she had converted the innocent piece of parchment into a perfect death-trap, rolled it up and replaced it, put back the rubber and pencil, and slipped out again on deck, where she sat down on a coil of rope and waited.

In another couple of minutes the boat was in the water, and the mate called rudely to Vaiti. She came without a word, covering her face with her dress, and sobbing bitterly. She stumbled as she walked; you would have sworn she was weak, broken in spirit, and utterly helpless.

If the mate felt any compassion, he did not dare to show it. They shoved off, two natives at the oars. Vaiti, sobbing effectively behind her hands, kept a sharp look-out with the corner of one eye as they slid across the dark water, but she could see nothing save a faintly glimmering line of grey shore, and hear nothing but the humming of the surf on the reef.

As soon as they reached the shallow water near the shore, the mate took Vaiti by her arm and roared, "Out you go!"

Sobbing afresh, in the most natural and convincing manner in the world, she obeyed.... It was dark, and the native who rowed bow oar never knew that she whipped his knife dexterously out of his belt as she passed him.

"Why are you marooning me?" she wailed, as she waded through the warm, shallow water towards the shore.

The mate leaned out of the boat, now fading fast away into the starry gloom, and shouted as he disappeared:

"To pay for Delgadas Reef and the *Margaret Macintyre!*"

Vaiti, who had reached the shore, almost sat down with the shock. So that was it! that was it! The pearl-shell lagoon out of which she, almost unaided, had "jockeyed" the schooner *Margaret Macintyre*, some months before, was bringing in a crop other than pearls—of which last, indeed, the canny Scot who had financed the working of the place had had very much the larger share.

Well, things must be taken as they were found. The soft tropic night stirred gently round her. The stars were large and golden; they shone in the still lagoon like little moons. Palm trees waved somewhere up in the dusk above, striking their huge rattling vanes together with the swing of the night-breeze. It was land, safe, solid land, and the sand was warm and soft, and Vaiti was tired. She walked a little way up the beach, stretched herself under a pandanus tree, and went to sleep....

Some hours later she woke, with the dim, mysterious volcano-glow of the tropic dawn in her eyes, and a curious feeling of disquiet about her heart. Still half asleep, she saw the long grey shore sloping down to the silent lagoon, the ink-coloured pandanus trees standing up against the dull orange sky, the leaning stems and stumps of coco-palms, dark and formless in the shadow. She shut her eyes and tried to sleep again.

No use. That nameless disquiet—now almost fear—still stirred at her heart. She opened her eyes once more, and looked about. A little more light—the touch of a glowing finger away in the east—a clearer defining of the cocoanut stumps, snapped off near their roots in the last great hurricane.... One of the stumps was oddly shaped—almost like a human figure. She could have fancied it was a rude image of a sitting man, only that the profile, against the lightening east, was featureless, and there was nothing to represent the hands.

"I will not be frightened by a rotten cocoanut tree," thought Vaiti. "I will sleep again till it is light. Am I not a sea-captain's daughter, and the descendant of great Island chiefs, and shall I fear the fancies of my own mind?"

Determinedly she closed her eyes again, and lay very still. The dawn wind began to stir; the ripples crisped upon the beach; the locusts in the trees broke out into a loud chirr-ing chorus. And as the day broke silver-clear upon the shore, Vaiti, still lying on the sand, felt that some one, in the gathering light, was watching her as she lay.

Wary as a fox, she opened her dark, keen eyes without stirring her body ... and looked straight into a face that was bending almost over her ... a face hooded by a black cloth that hid the head and brow, and only left to view ... O God! O God! what was it?

The thing was featureless. Nose, eyes, and mouth were gone. In the midst of a cavern of unspeakable ruin the ghastly throat gaped vacant. Two handless, rotting stumps of arms waved blindly about—feeling—feeling....

Could it hear? Some instinct told the girl that it could. Softly as a snake she writhed out of the reach of those terrible groping arms.

It did hear. It sprang blindly forward—it snatched.

With one leap Vaiti was on her feet. Never looking back, she fled down the open beach, the sand spurting behind her as she ran. She heard a dull padding in her rear at first; it soon grew faint, but she ran on blindly, long after it had died away—ran, while the sun climbed over the horizon and cast down handfuls of burning gold on her uncovered head—ran, while the beach grew parchment-white and dazzled back the heat into her face like an open furnace—ran till at last her over-driven body gave way, and the sand spun round and the sky turned red before her eyes. Then only she staggered into the shade and dropped down upon a green mattress of convolvulus creeper to rest.

And now, when she had leisure to think and strength to cast off the haunting horror of that inhuman face, she knew what Donahue had done.

This was not Bilboa, the uninhabited guano island that she had feared. This was infinitely worse—it was Vaka, the leper isle!

She remembered that she had once heard a dim rumour of Vaka and its ghastly leper people—the remnant of a plague-smitten tribe long ago forcibly exiled there from one of the fierce western groups. No ships ever called at this graveyard of the living; it was supposed that the cocoanuts and fish of the island provided sufficient food for the people, and no one cared to run the chance of their stowing away and escaping, especially as they were known to be both daring and treacherous on occasion. Donahue had indeed laid his plans well for the most hideous revenge that the heart of man or devil could conceive. A few weeks or months in this charnel-house of horrors, where the very air must reek of contagion, and what would it avail her if, after all, some stray, storm-driven vessel should rescue the castaway? Better, then, that she should stay and die among the other nameless nightmare horrors that walked these stricken shores.

No! Vaiti, sitting cross-legged on the netted vines and staring grimly out to sea, then and there took resolve that such a fate should not be hers.... Sharks were uncertain, if you really wanted them; but the stick of dynamite she had taken from the mate's cabin was safe and sure. If she failed in using it for the special purpose she had planned, she would put it in her mouth and light the fuse.... There would be no more trouble after that. And as for the flies—one did not feel them, of course, when one was dead.

All the same, she did not mean to die if she could avoid it, and, as the first step towards helping herself, she knocked some nuts off a young palm, and took her breakfast off the refreshing water and juicy meat. Then she cut a length of bush rope, looped it round the tallest palm in sight, and set her feet inside the loop, so that she could work herself up to the top of the tree, monkey-on-stick fashion, leaning against the rope. When she got into the crown of the palm she knelt among the leaves, holding on tightly, and looked right and left over the island.

It was a pure atoll, an irregular circle of feather palms lying on the sea like a great green garland set afloat. The inner lagoon was several square miles in extent, but the land was not more than a few hundred yards wide at any point, and there was no soil to speak of. The palms, the scanty, pale green scrub, the mop-headed pandanus trees, the trailing creepers, all sprang out of pure white coral gravel and sand. The scene was lovely as only a coral atoll can be—the jewel-green water of the inner lagoon, shaded with vivid reflections of lilac and pale turquoise, the stately circled palms, the wide, white beach enclasping all the island like a frame of purest pearl, the burning blue of the surrounding sea, all combined to form a picture bright as fairyland and sparkling as an enamelled gem set upon a velvet shield.

But Vaiti, while she saw and admired the loveliness of the scene, also recognised its barrenness as only an islander could. No fruit, no roots, little fresh water—nothing, in fact, but cocoanut and pandanus kernels, eked out by a little fish.... The lepers must often go hungry.

The hot day turned suddenly chill as Vaiti recalled those blind, snatching, handless arms. They came of a cannibal race, these Vaka folk. What if she had not waked? What if, wearied as she well might be, she slept too long and too soundly in the night that was to come?

# CHAPTER VII

## THE TURNING OF THE TABLES

She looked narrowly about the island, hoping to discover the place where the lepers lived. A cluster of small, miserable huts, on the far side of the lagoon, attracted her attention. It seemed not more than half a mile from the spot where she had spent the night. The best fishing grounds she judged, by the look of the shore, to be near the village. She was therefore, no doubt, several miles from their usual haunts.

So far, so good. Where was the schooner? It lay to her left about a mile out at sea, close to a small, uninhabited, sandy islet. Vaiti supposed that the men were cutting wood and looking for water. She saw one or two black dots on the shore, recognisable by their blue dungaree clothing, and strained her eyes eagerly to see if the dinghy had been pulled up on the sand, for in this lay her only chance. If they brought the boat up on the beach, to repair her where wood could be had without going to the atoll itself (Vaiti would have wagered that the *Ikurangi* did not carry a splinter outside of the galley fuel), then the schooner would probably stop overnight. In that case she could carry out her plans. Otherwise ... there was always the dynamite.

The dinghy was ashore, drawn well up on the beach.

She drew a breath of relief, and slid down the tree again. Now she could wait till night with an easy mind.

All day she hid in the tangle of young palm and low-growing scrub that clustered about the foot of the loftier trees. Once she saw a couple of the lepers pass by in the distance, evidently looking for something. These had eyes, and she crept closer into the shelter of the scrub till they were gone. Then she came cautiously out, and plucked long sheets of the fine pale-brown natural matting that protects the young shoot of the cocoanut, to cover up her white dress, for the scrub was dangerously thin, in that staring overhead sun. She did not venture down to the sea to fish, but fed upon cocoanuts during the day.

Night came at last—night and coolness, with big stars shining in the lagoon, and a gentle breeze stirring among the palms. About midnight, as near as she could guess, Vaiti came out of her shelter and prepared for action.

She took off her clothes, and fastened about her waist a petticoat of the dark-coloured cocoanut matting which she had stitched together during the day. So habited, with her olive skin and black hair, she knew that she was invisible in the darkness of the night. She fastened the dynamite, and a box of matches, into the coil of hair on the top of her head, stuck her knife into the waist of her petticoat, and walked down the beach into the warm, dark sea.

She knew very well that the outer side of an atoll commonly swarms with sharks, but the risk did not trouble her. There was something a good deal worse to face on the island than any number of sharks. Heading for the distant light of the schooner, she swam through the starry water with the low, dog-like island paddle that can cover such marvellous distances—keeping her head well out, and quietly taking her time.

It was a long swim, but it ended at last, and the schooner rose up before her in the water, black and silent, and shifting ever so little upon the swell of the incoming tide. The stars made little trickles of light upon her wet, dark hull. Two boats lay alongside—the dinghy, freshly mended and watertight, and the whaleboat, loaded with wood and cocoanuts. After the slovenly fashion of the *Ikurangi*, they had left the boats until the morning to hoist inboard, seeing that it was dead calm in the lee of the islet.

This was more than Vaiti had hoped for, and it made her task easy. She cut the dinghy's painter, got into the boat, and muffled the oars with a strip or two torn from her petticoat. Then she put the dynamite into the whaleboat, cut and attached a good long fuse, set a match to it, and saw that the tiny red spark was steadily eating its way along, before she pulled off from the ship. She towed the whaleboat after her a little way, and then let it go thirty or forty yards from the ship. It was not her desire to wreck the schooner at Vaka Island, and possibly let loose her enemies upon the atoll; rather she wished the ship well out of the way before any disaster should overtake her. The charts would most probably ensure that matter. The destruction of the boat was only intended to secure her own possession of the dinghy.

She had scarcely reached the shore before a loud explosion boomed out across the water, and immediately after lights began to stir on board the schooner. Vaiti worked with coolness and speed, knowing that it was not likely, though possible, that any one would swim ashore. From her eyrie in the coco-palm she had noted a deep, narrow creek running up from the lagoon—a mere crack in the coral, but wide enough to admit a small boat, taken in with care. There was just enough light from the stars to enable her to find the place, and run the boat up on the sand at the end, into the heart of a tangle of leaves and creepers that entirely concealed it. For safety's sake, she cut a few more armfuls of trailing vines from the shore, and buried the boat two or three feet deep, so that neither from the sea nor the land could it possibly be seen.

As she worked, she could hear shouts and cries, made faint by distance, coming across the water from the schooner. She could imagine the scene that would take place on board when they found themselves boatless. Some of the native crew—not Donahue or the mate; they would never face the sharks—would probably swim ashore to-morrow to investigate. Well, let them!

Having finished the concealing of the dinghy, she got into it herself, put on her clothes again, drew the tangled creepers well over her, and went calmly to sleep, secure that no one could find her unless she chose to be found.

All the same, she was very cautious about getting up the next morning, and looked carefully between the leaves before she ventured out of her hiding-place. She covered up her light dress with the cocoanut canvas, and then climbed a palm to look about.

People were moving hurriedly about the decks of the schooner; something seemed to be going on. As she watched, she saw two natives, clad only in loin-cloths, stand up on the bulwarks, ready to dive. In another moment they had flashed down into the sea, small as ants to sight at that distance, but perfectly clear to Vaiti's sea-trained eyes. Then the dark specks began to make their way across the water. The sun was newly risen, the sea was still a mirror of molten gold, and the tiny black heads stood out sharply on its surface. Vaiti set her teeth as she watched them creeping on. They were island men, of her mother's own race, and they had done her no harm. And ... the longer a vessel lies at anchor in equatorial latitudes, the more certain it is that sharks will gather round her—even if there has been no explosion in the water alongside to kill the fish and collect the tigers of the sea from far and near.

Vaiti looked away, and began desperately to count the nuts clustered among the palm-fronds at her feet.... How many were there? Ten—fifteen—twenty——

A long, despairing shriek tore across the water. She put her fingers in her ears and buried her face in the leaves. Yet, all the same, she heard a second cry, short and sudden, and quickly ended. There was nothing more. She lifted her face again, her teeth set tight into her lower lip. The two black heads were gone.

"No one will come ashore to-day," she said, with a shiver. Something seemed to stab her, as she thought of that doctored chart in the schooner's deck cabin. The reefs on the course to South America were hundreds of miles from shore—the ship had no boats—and the native crew must suffer with the villainous captain and mate, if the disaster that she had plotted so carefully should come about.... There would be sharks there, too, when the ship broke up....

The crystal-gold of the sea turned dim before Vaiti's eyes. It was only a mist of tears that lay between, but to the girl's excited imagination it seemed like the spreading and darkening stain of blood.

Careless of whether she was seen or not, she slid down the tree and rushed into the scrub, where she sat down upon the sand and cried like a mere nervous schoolgirl. The sun was past the zenith when she lifted her head again; the schooner had put out to sea, and lay, a far-off snowy speck, upon the blue horizon.

Vaiti stood up, flung back her hair, and cast the trouble from her. She could not afford to grieve over the inevitable now; there was too much to do. The boat had to be prepared and provisioned, and that was not the work of a moment.

She husked and opened a number of large cocoanuts, and removed the insides. She then cut a quantity of young palm-leaves, and plaited them into baskets, which she filled with the cocoanut meat. Afterwards she cut down dozens of young green nuts for drinking, husked them to save space, and slung them together in bunches with strips of their own fibre. This done, she hid the provisions in the boat, and set about her own supper, as it was almost dark.

Nourishing food she felt she must have, if she was to get through with her enterprise, but she dared not attract attention to herself by going out torch-fishing on the reef. However, there were certain holes in the ground about the roots of the palms that to her experienced eye promised something better than fish.

She dug a fire-hole in the gravel at the end of the gully where she had hidden the boat, lined it with stones, and made a fire, looking well to it that no gleam should be visible from above. When the stones were beginning to heat, she took a piece of palms-leaf in her hand, hid herself in the bush, and waited, still as a rock.

By-and-by there was a faint scuffling among the roots of the trees, and a shadowy thing began climbing up the trunk of a palm. Vaiti waited till it had disappeared in the crown of the tree, and then climbed after it to a point about ten feet from the top, where she tied her strip of leaf round the trunk and came down again.

Thump! thump! Two cocoanuts fell to the earth. The crab (for it was a cocoanut crab of the biggest and fiercest kind) was getting his supper. Now he would come down the tree, rip open the nuts with his formidable claws, and enjoy the contents.

Slowly he began to back down the palm, his sensitive tail ready to tell him when he had touched earth and might safely let go. And now it was that Vaiti's trap (a well-known native trick) proved his undoing. The belt of dry leaflets round the tree tickled his tail, he promptly let go, and fell with a crash seventy feet through air on to the pile of coral lumps that Vaiti had heaped up at the foot of the tree.

The girl picked him up, badly injured and unable to use his claws (which were big enough to crack her ankle), and put an end to him with a clever stroke of her knife. He proved to be two feet long in the body alone, and of a fine blue and red colour, as seen in the dim light of the fire. She put him on the heated stones, wrapped in leaves, buried him until cooked, and then enjoyed a hot supper that an epicure might have envied.

Strengthened by the good food, she worked on late into the night, catching more crabs, whose meat she hoped she could dry in the sun, making a rough sail out of the bed-sheet she had carried away from the schooner, twisting sinnet plait out of cocoanut husk for ropes, cutting and trimming a small pandanus for the mast. She had all her plans laid, and knew what she meant to do. Her present position was about five hundred miles from the Marquesas, and the south-east trades would be in her favour. With lines for fishing, a beaker full of fresh water on board (she had found that in the dinghy when she took it away), cocoanuts to help out with, and plenty of crab to dry, she hoped that she might manage to reach the islands before her strength or her food gave out. Greater voyages had been done many a time in mere canoes, and the dinghy was a large boat of its kind, strong, well built, and new. If she failed—well, any death, any horror that the wide seas could hold was better than Vaka Island.

All being ready, she lay down and slept till dawn—a somewhat restless sleep, for it was full of wandering dreams, and all the dreams took one shape: Donahue's schooner, snared by the lying chart, rushing helpless to her end, with the green-eyed tigers of the sea hovering ever about the reefs, and waiting ... waiting....

*     *     *     *     *

"I don't think the patient can see any one," said the nurse doubtfully.

The big, yellow-haired sailor took off his hat and stepped up on to the verandah. It was a very beautiful verandah. You could see most of Suva Bay from it, and half the tumbled purple peaks of Fiji's wonderful mountains lying across the harbour.

"If you could stretch a point, ma'am," said the sailor, "it might be as well for him. I've got good news."

"About his daughter?" asked the nurse. She, like every one else in Suva, was deeply interested in this especial patient's story. He had come to Suva in his own schooner, the *Sybil*, several weeks before, furious with rage and despair at the loss of his daughter, and eager to demand assistance from the High

Commissioner of the Western Pacific, although it seemed by no means clear in what manner Her Majesty's representative could aid him. Before the matter had even been discussed, however, he had fallen seriously ill of sunstroke and excitement combined, and had been sent to hospital, with rather a bad chance of recovery. He was just turning the corner now, and the nurse—who could not but admire his rather weather-beaten good looks and romantic history—regarded him as her most interesting patient.

"Yes, it's about his daughter," answered the sailor. "I'm the mate of the *Sybil*, ma'am; Harris is my name. Perhaps you'd kindly read this."

He held out a long slip of printed paper, containing a *résumé* of the cables for the day—Suva's substitute for a daily paper.

The nurse took it, and read:

"The missing daughter of Edward Saxon, owner and master of the trading schooner *Sybil*, has at last reappeared. Her fate has excited much interest and conjecture all over the Pacific. She arrived in Sydney yesterday on board the cable-ship *Clotho*, by which she was picked up on the 2nd instant, in an open boat, alone, and two hundred miles from any land. She had experienced bad weather, and was much exhausted for want of food, but declared herself capable, if it had been necessary, of reaching the nearest island group unaided. She had been carried away, as was surmised, by the captain of the island schooner *Ikurangi*, who marooned her on a remote leper island, Vaka, and then sailed for South America. Revenge for the loss of a pearl-shell bed of disputed ownership is said to have been the motive of this unparalleled outrage."

"He shall have it at once," said the nurse cordially. "It'll do him more good than our medicines."

\*     \*     \*     \*     \*

The story was a popular one in the hospital for months after, and it had not been quite forgotten when, towards the close of the hot season, a Sydney paper furnished the last chapter of the tale. Saxon's late nurse read it aloud to the others at afternoon tea, and they all agreed (not knowing how Vaiti's fingers had cogged the dice of chance) that it was a wonderful Providence and a real judgment. The item read:

"THE LAST OF AN OCEAN ROMANCE.

"News comes via Tahiti from Nukahiva, Marquesas Islands, of the arrival of a shipwrecked crew on a raft, six weeks ago. They were the survivors of a disaster that destroyed the notorious schooner *Ikurangi* whose master, it will be remembered, kidnapped and marooned the daughter of a British captain some months ago. The schooner, after leaving the island, sailed for Callao, but was wrecked on an uncharted reef three days east of Vaka, and went to pieces. The crew escaped on a raft, and underwent great suffering in their efforts to reach land. The captain and mate were drowned."

"And serve them right, too!" said the audience.

# CHAPTER VIII

## THE WHITE MAN OF NALOLO

"By Jove! it's a white man," said Saxon, checking like a pointer on the threshold of the low dark doorway.

"Certainly. Very pleased to meet you," observed the figure on the mats. It was sitting cross-legged, clad only in a waist-cloth, and the house was a Fijian chief-house in a mountain village three days' journey from the nearest white settlement—but the thing squatted on the mats was undoubtedly white, and—English? Well, no; Saxon thought no. The phrase was American in flavour. He stepped across the threshold, and came a little way in, relieved in mind. When you have been dead and buried among the islands for a quarter of a century it is much pleasanter not to run the risk of meeting other ghosts (with university accents, tea-coloured families, and a preference for modest retirement on steamer days) who may possibly have been alive together with you before....

Before.... The word means much in that vast Pacific world, sepulchre of so many lost hopes and forgotten lives. We do not, in the Islands, cultivate curiosity as a virtue, since it would be likely to bring rather more than virtue's own reward after it. We do not ask cross questions, because the crooked answers might involve questions of another sort. And when overfed, sanguineous passengers from smart liners happen along and tell us, as a new and excellent joke, that the proper formula for receiving an introduction in the Islands is: "Glad to meet you, Mr. So-and-so; what were you called *before?*" we smile an acid smile, and pretend we are amused....

Saxon was very tired, having walked thirty miles that day, and very hungry, being out of luck, and more or less on the tramp. But I think, tired as he was, he would have found another village to rest in if the derelict white on the mats had spoken with the shibboleth of his own class and country.

As things were, the look of the house pleased him, and he came in and folded himself up on the mats. The other man noted that he selected a "tabu kaisi" mat (a kind strictly forbidden to all but chiefs or whites), and that he looked hopefully towards the kava bowl.

"Not the first time you've stopped under a pandanus roof, I guess?" he remarked.

"No," said Saxon. "Whose house is this?"

"Mine," said the stranger. "Make yourself at home."

It was a handsome chief-house of the best Fijian type, forty feet from mats to ridge-pole, the walls covered with beautifully inlaid and interwoven reeds, the roof bound together with exquisite sinnet work in artistic patterns, of red, black, and yellow, and towering up into a dark, cool cavern of pleasant gloom. The floor was overlaid with fine parquetry of split bamboo at the "kasii" or common-folk end, and piled deep with fine mats in the "chief" part. A Fijian bed, ten feet wide and three feet high, ran like a dais right across the end of the house. It was covered by mats prettily fringed with coloured parrot feathers. There were three great doors, east, west, and south, each framing in its dark-set opening a different picture of surpassing loveliness. Nalolo town (its name is on the map of Fiji, but it reads otherwise) stands very high on the sheer crest of a pointed green hill that is just like the enchanted hill in the pictures of a fairy tale. There is a little round green lawn on the top, and all about it stand the high, pointed beehive houses of the town, each perched on its own tiny mound like a toy on a stand. Sloped cocoanut logs run up to the doors of the houses, and quaintly coloured crotons cluster about them. In the deep, soft grass golden eggs from the guava trees lie tumbled about among fallen stars of orange and lemon blossom, and everywhere the red hibiscus shakes its splendid bells in the soft hill-winds. About the foot of the peak a wide blue river wanders, singing all day long; and from every door of every house, high perched above the cloudy valleys and hyacinth hill ranges, one can see pictures, and pictures, and pictures almost too lovely to be true. There are not two places in the world like Nalolo.

The White Man of Nalolo, however, was only interested in the fact that the river provided excellent crayfish; and that taro grew very well indeed on the slopes below the town. He had once been young, but he was not young now, and did not matter any longer. Therefore he had become particular about his dinner and indifferent to scenery. I will not tell you the story of the White Man of Nalolo, or why he, of all men, rebelled so fiercely against the common lot of "not mattering any more," that he came away to the wilds of the Pacific and the highlands of Fiji, and never went back again, because, like many true stories, it cannot be believed, and therefore had better not be told. Besides, this is the story of Saxon and his daughter.

Saxon was down on his luck. He had a charter for the *Sybil*, but she was not able to undertake it at present, for, trying to pilot her into Suva harbour himself, he had contrived to run her on a reef, and damaged her so seriously that she was at present careened on the beach in front of the local boat-builder's, undergoing repairs. The builder, knowing something of Saxon's reputation, had insisted on cash in advance, and the captain, in consequence, found himself so nearly out of funds that he was unable to stay in Suva pending the repairs to his ship. He had therefore started with Vaiti for the interior of the great island of Viti Levu, intending to live on the real hospitality of the natives for a few weeks, and tramp from village to village.

He explained something of this as he sat on the mats enjoying the grateful coolness of the house. The other man nodded gravely, watching the door. He offered a curious contrast to the Englishman's coarse red fairness, being lean, sundried, and grizzled, with expressionless, boot-buttoned eyes, and a straggling "goatee" beard that dated his exile from America back to long-ago days.

"Where's your daughter?" he asked.

"Coming. She stopped to tidy up at the river."

The doorway was darkened at that moment by Vaiti herself, balancing lightly up the cocoanut log to the threshold. She wore a white tunic over a scarlet "pareo," her wavy curls, sparkling with the water of the stream, fell loose upon her shoulders; her lips were as red as the freshly-plucked pomegranate blossom behind her ear. Something like life stirred in the boot-button eyes of the White Man of Nalolo as he looked at her.

"Afi!" he called to a Fijian woman who was sleeping on the mats at the "kaisi" end of the house, "go and hurry the girls with the supper, and make tea for the marama (lady). Quick!"

Then he turned to Saxon.

"Stay here as long as you like, both of you," he said. "Let her sit there sometimes, where I can see her and fancy.... I'll show you something."

He rose slowly and stiffly, and limped across to a Chinese camphorwood box that stood in the corner. In a minute he returned with a faded photograph in a gaudy frame.

"My daughter," he said. "The only child I ever had. She was Afi's. She died a long time ago. Afi's a chief woman: she was as handsome as Andi Thakombau when she was young, and the girl took after her. Your girl's mother was chief too, I guess. Do you see any likeness?"

Vaiti and her father craned over the photograph. The pretty half-caste girl, was certainly like the stately, slender creature who gazed at her pictured face, though the fire and spirit of Vaiti's expression were wanting.

"I'm growing old," went on the White Man. "I've no children. Stay a bit. I'll be glad to have you."

"Thank you; delighted, I'm sure," drawled Saxon, with a pathetic resurrection of his long-forgotten "grand manner," And so it was settled.

Vaiti, listening and thinking as usual, with her chin in her slender fingers, approved of what she heard, and smiled very pleasantly at her host. It seemed to her that he could be very useful just now.

The four weeks that followed after glided away agreeably enough in the silent hills. Nothing happened; no one came or went—the Fijians, men and women, went out to the yam and taro fields in the morning, and returned in the afternoon; and after dark there would be long, monotonous chanting, and interminable sitting dances, on the mats inside the high-roofed houses. Saxon stupefied himself with kava most of the time, in the absence of stronger drink, and almost got himself clubbed once or twice on account of his too impulsive admiration for the beauties of the village. His host, however, was no censor of morals, and troubled very little about him. On Sundays the Fijians dressed themselves in their brightest cottons, stuck up their hair in huge halos, and went five times to church, under the auspices of the native Wesleyan teacher; while Saxon and his host smoked, slept, drank kava, and played cards. The village provided plenty of yam and taro, kumara, cocoanut, and fish; and there was tea and sugar in the Chinese box, and now and then the White Man killed a pig or a fowl. It was very pleasant on the whole.

In a month's time, however, Saxon girded up his loins to leave this mountain Capua and descend to Suva once more. The *Sybil* would be ready, and his charter to convey ornamental Fiji woods to San Francisco would not wait.

They said good-bye to their host, and walked a mile or two across the river-flats below the town before either spoke. Then Vaiti put her hand into her sash, and drew out something small and shining.

"See, father, what the White Man gave me, because I was like his daughter," she said.

Saxon took the object, and turned it over in his fingers. It was a small seal, shaped like an eagle standing on a rock. The eagle was gold, the rock amethyst.

"A pretty thing, but not worth more than two or three pounds," he said.

Then he turned it over and looked at the device. There was a curious crest on the face of the seal—a wolf with a crescent moon in his jaws; underneath, a motto in a strange foreign character.

Saxon's red complexion paled as he examined the crest. In other days and scenes, among ice-bound rivers and grim mediæval fortress-castles, he had seen that crest light up the crimson panes of old armorial windows—had read the motto underneath—"What I have, I hold"—of nights when he and the wildest young nobles of the Russian court were dining together under the splendid roof of one of Moscow's greatest banqueting halls. For a moment he felt the keen cold air of the ice-bound streets blow sharp on his cheek; heard the jingle of the sleigh-bells, drawing up before the marble steps where the yellow lamplight streamed out across the snow. The fancy faded, swift as a passing lantern picture that flashes out for a moment and then sweeps away into darkness. He saw the burning sky and the crackling palms again, felt the furnace-heated wind, and knew that it was all over long ago, and that he was ruined, exiled, and old. Yet there remained a thread of indefinite recollection, a suggestion of something half-remembered, that was not all unconnected with the present day. What was the story belonging to that crest—the story that the whole world knew?

"Where did the fellow get the thing?" he asked his daughter.

Vaiti told him.

The White Man of Nalolo, it seemed, was one of the numerous South Sea wanderers who believe in the existence of various undiscovered islands, hidden here and there in the vast, untravelled wastes of sea that lie off the track of ships. Thirty years before, there had been wondering rumours of an island of this kind, touched at once by a ship that no one could name, found to be uninhabited, and never revisited; indeed, no one was sure where it was within a few hundred miles. Years went by, and the White Man, who had always taken a special interest in the story, found himself shipwrecked—the sole survivor of a boatful of castaways—on the very island itself. But fortune was unkind, for the morning after his arrival, when he was trying to sail round the island, a sudden storm blew him out to sea again, and he had drifted for many days, and all but perished, in spite of the fish and nuts he had obtained from the island, before a mission schooner happened to see him and pick him up. He had examined most of the island while ashore, and had seen no inhabitants or traces of cultivation. Nevertheless he had always been convinced that there was something mysterious about the place, for two reasons. One was the presence of common house-flies, which he had never seen far away from the haunts of human beings. The other was the discovery of an amethyst seal, lying under a stone on the shore. It was dirty and discoloured, but he did not think so small and heavy an object could have been washed up on the shore from a wreck.

Where mystery is in the air, most men's minds turn naturally to thoughts of hidden treasure, and the White Man of Nalolo had ever since cherished a hope that there was treasure on the island. For several years he had fully intended to go and look—some day—but as he could only guess at the latitude and longitude, and as he had little money to spare, he never succeeded either in hunting the place up himself or in persuading any one else to do so. Now he was old and half-crippled, and did not care any more about anything; so he wanted Vaiti, who reminded him so much of his dead daughter, to have the seal. It was a pretty thing, and perhaps it would make her think sometimes of the poor old White Man of Nalolo.

Saxon listened attentively to the story, and heaved a sigh of disappointment at the end.

"There's nothing in it, my girl," he said. "No proof of treasure there, eh?"

"No; no treasure," said Vaiti, looking at the ground as she walked.

"What then?" asked Saxon curiously. He saw she had something in reserve.

Vaiti suddenly flamed out in eloquent Maori.

"What then, my father? Am I one who sees through men's heads, that I can tell what was in the mind of you as you looked at the jewel, and turned yellow and green like a parrot, only to see it? What then? I do not know. I walk in the dark, and the light is in your hand, not in mine. As for you, you have made your brain dull with the brandy and the kava, so that you cannot see at all. What then? Tell me yourself, for I do not know. I know only that there is something to be told."

"Don't be rough on your poor old father," said Saxon pathetically. "I'd have knocked the stuffing out of any man who said half as much, but I spoil you, by Gad, I do. I don't know—I can't think, somehow or other. But there was a story about the Vasilieffs—the johnnies who had that crest—people I used to stay with when I went to——"

He broke off, smashed a spider-lily bloom with his stick, and began afresh.

"Junia Vasilieff—what was it she did? Big princes they were, and much too close to the throne to be safe company.... Junia Vasili—I have it! Yes—the end of the story was in the Sydney papers, time you were a little kid. I remember. They were to have married her to the Czarewitch, just to make things safe. Her claim to the throne was big enough to have started a revolution any day, if it had been asserted.... Poor little Junia!—only sixteen when I knew—when the marriage was talked of—and such golden hair as she had! She hated the whole thing; courts and ceremony weren't in her line. But she was a gentle little creature, and I never thought she'd have had the spirit to do as she did."

He turned the seal over in his fingers, as if reading the past from its glittering surface.

"There was a young lieutenant of Hussars, a Pole—you don't know what that is, but the Russians don't like them, I can tell you—a noble, but a very small one; not fit to black Junia's boots, according to their notions. Well, he bolted with her. It was in the Sydney papers, time I was in the Solomons; the paper came up to Guadalcanar.... She must have been twenty then; just the year the marriage to the Czarewitch was to have come off.... They bolted—cleared out—never seen again. All Russia on the boil about it; no one knew but what they'd hatch up plots against the throne, she having a better claim than any one else, if it hadn't been for the law against empresses. The secret police were after them for years, but they were never traced, though most people knew Russia'd give a pretty penny to know where they were——"

"O man with the head of a fruit-bat, do you not see?" interrupted Vaiti at this juncture. "They hid on that island—they may be there still. It is worth a hundred treasures!"

"The Pole was a great traveller, and had a sort of a little yacht," said Saxon thoughtfully. "It might be true, of course—if there is an island, and if the Nalolo Johnnie had any idea of where it was, and if nobody found them out and split years ago. Plenty of 'ifs.'"

"I think him all-right good enough," averred Vaiti, returning to English and prose. "By'n-by we finish F'lisco, then we go see, me and you."

# CHAPTER IX

## THE LOST ISLAND

Some two or three months later, the schooner might have been seen, like a white-winged butterfly lost at sea, beating up and down before a solitary, low, green island lying far east of the lonely Paumotus. Vaiti, sitting on the top of the deck-house, was examining the land through a glass. The native crew were all on deck; also Harris and Gray, the mate and bo'sun. Captain Saxon was not to be seen.

"The old man always do get squiffy at the wrong time, don't he?" commented Harris, rather gleefully.

Gray spat over the rail for reply.

"You're ratty because you don't know nothing, ain't you?" he said.

"Do you?" asked the mate curiously. Harris had not much notion of the dignity of his office, and dearly loved a gossip at all times.

"More nor you, havin' eyes and ears that's of use to me occasionally," replied the bo'sun dryly.

Harris considered.

"I'll give you my grey shirt to tell," he said persuasively. "There's sure to be something up."

"'Ow much does we ever get out of it when there is?" asked Gray sourly. "I could do with that shirt very well, though. There ain't much to tell, except that the old man he thought there was an island hereabouts not marked on the chart that nobody knew about; and Vaiti she allowed that was all —— rot, because, says she, this part's been surveyed, and though the Admiralty surveys isn't the for-ever-'n-ever-Amen dead certainties the little brassbound officers thinks them, still they don't leave whole islands out on the loose without a collar and a name round their necks, so to say. So, says she, let me work out the length of time they ran before the hurricane, says she, and the d'rection of the wind, which the old boy remembered right enough, says she; and then look it up on the chart, and I'll be blowed, says she, if you don't find something for a guide like. So by-and-by she looks, and says she, ''Ere's something; 'ere's a reef marked P.D., and it is P.D.,' says she, 'for you and I knows there's nothin' there,' she says. 'But we'll look a bit more to the north'ard,' she says, 'where it's right off the' track of ships, and maybe we'll find somethin' and maybe we won't,' she says. 'But I think,' she says, 'that somewheres not too far off from that P.D. reef we'll maybe get a sight of what we're lookin' for,' she says, 'because sometimes reefs is put down for bigger things by mistake,' she says, 'especially if you 'aven't been to see.' Then she comes on deck, and I makes myself scarce, for it ain't healthy on this ship to listen at no cabin skylights, not if she knows you're there."

"Well, whatever the game is, I don't suppose it'll line our little insides any fatter, bo'sun. We don't count on this ship anything like as we ought to when there's shares goin'. I wonder that I stick to her, I do! Old man as drunk as a lord half the time—me doin' his work as well as my own—a blessed she-cat running the blooming show——"

"Ready about!" sang Vaiti from the deck-house, and the mate and bo'sun sprang across the deck. There was something about the orders of the "she-cat" that enforced a smartness on the *Sybil* rare on an island schooner, even when heavy-fisted Saxon was not about.

Half an hour later, Vaiti had rowed herself ashore, curtly declining Harris's polite offers of assistance, and had landed on the beach. As she did not know who she might be going to see, she had provided for all emergencies. Her revolver was in her pocket, and she wore a flowing sacque of lace-trimmed white silk that made her feel she was fit to meet any Russian princess, if such were indeed on the island. It was a gratifying thought that the said princess, if she had been a celebrated beauty, must now be well into the forties, and consequently beneath all contempt as a rival belle.

Her father's absence did not trouble her. He had a nasty trick of starting a drinking bout just when he was most needed—in fact, it was the one point in Saxon's character on which you could absolutely rely. Vaiti, therefore, had grown used to doing without him, and rather liked to have a perfectly free hand.

She had fully grasped the bearings of the case. There was possibly a very great chief's daughter from Europe, with a rather insignificant chief who had stolen her away, living there in hiding. The people of her country would pay a great deal to know where she was and bring her back. Or, if there seemed any lack of safety about this proceeding (Vaiti had long ago learned that her father was not fond of putting himself within the reach of principalities and powers of any kind), the couple themselves must be made to pay for silence. It was all very simple.

The fact that the island was supposed to be uninhabited did not trouble her. She meant to investigate that matter after her own fashion.

She walked all round it first of all. It took her about an hour. There was a nice, white, sandy beach, with straggling bush behind it. There were a good many cocoanuts—all young ones—also a large number of broken trunks, apparently snapped off by a hurricane.

This set Vaiti thinking. It seemed to her that the damage was rather too universal and even to be natural. Yet why should any sane human cut short all his full-grown cocoanuts?

She crossed the island twice at the ends, noting everything with a keen and wary eye. Fairly good soil; nothing growing on it, however, but low scrub and a few berries. In the centre of the island the scrub thickened into dense bush, impenetrable without an axe. No sign of life anywhere.

Vaiti stamped her foot. Was it possible she had been mistaken? Was this indeed just what it seemed, a commonplace, infertile, useless, little mid-ocean islet, let alone because it was worth nothing, and incorrectly described as a reef because no one had ever troubled to examine it? Things began to look like it.

And yet ... she thought—she did not quite know what, but she was very sure that she did not want to leave the island just yet. She would at least climb a tall tree and take a general survey before she gave it up.

Nothing simpler—but there was no such tree.

All the palms were young, or broken off short; all the pandanus trees were in the same condition. There was no rock, no commanding height. She could not get a view.

Vaiti's cheek flushed crimson under its olive brown. The spark was struck at last!

Somebody had cut short those trees—to prevent anyone from climbing up and overlooking the island. The encircling reef would not allow any ship to approach close enough for a look-out at the mast-head to see over the island, except in a very general way. There was something to conceal. What, and where?

Only one answer was possible. The mass of apparently virgin bush in the centre of the island—several acres in extent—was the only spot where a cat could have concealed itself. The scent was growing hot.

With sparkling eyes Vaiti began to circle the wood, watching narrowly for the smallest trace of a pathway. The branches were interlocked and knitted together as only tropical bush can be. Many were set with huge thorns; all were laced and twined with bush ropes and lianas of every kind.

Nothing larger than a rat could have won its way through such a rampart. Vaiti walked swiftly on and on, striking the bushes now and then with a stick, to make sure that there were no loose masses of stuff masking a concealed entrance, and keeping a sharp eye for traces of footsteps.... It was with a heart-sinking shock that she found herself once more beside the low white coral rock that had marked the commencement of her journey, and realised that she had been all round, and that there was most certainly no opening.

The sun was slipping down the heavens now. She had been exploring half the day, but she was not beaten yet. The unexpected difficulties she had met with only sharpened her determination to enter the thicket at all costs. Harris, suffering acutely, as usual, from suppressed curiosity, was nearly driven mad by the sight of the "she-cat" suddenly reappearing on the ship, picking up an axe, and departing as silently as she had come, with a countenance that did not invite questions. She had taken off her smart silk dress, and was in her chemise and petticoat, arms and feet bare, and waist girdled with a sash into which she had stuck her revolver. She dropped the axe into her boat, rowed silently away, and disappeared on the other side of the island.

The sun was still some distance above the sea when she let the axe slip from her torn, scratched, and aching hands, and stood at last, tired but triumphant, in the heart of the mysterious island's mystery. She had won her way, with the woodcraft that was in her island blood, through the dense belt of bush, hacking and slashing here, stooping and writhing there, until the light began to show through the tangled stems in front, and a few swift strokes cleared the way into the open. Yes! there was a space in the centre, after all—a clearing over an acre in extent. There was grass here, and a few overgrown bananas, and a tangle of yam and pumpkin vines. Passion fruit ran in a tangle of wild luxuriance over the inner wall of the thicket; pine-apples rotted on the ground and fig-trees spread their wide leaves unchecked and unpruned.... In the middle of all was a house—a one-storied little bungalow, iron-roofed, with a tank to catch the rain. There was a long, low store behind it, and something that looked like a pig-sty, and something that might have been a fowl-run. But....

But everything was rotten, ruined, overgrown, hardly to be distinguished in the thick tangle of vegetation that had overflowed the little retreat like a great green wave let loose upon a low-lying shore. Vaiti knew what she was going to see before she had reached the door of the bungalow—a rotten floor, with green vines shooting up between the crevices, and bush rats scuffling and squeaking under the boards—a rusted iron roof, where pink convolvulus bloom peeped in under the rafters, and lizards sunned themselves in the airy blue furniture unglued and decayed fast sinking into one common mass of ruin—door aslant, and thresholds sunken. Everywhere silence, emptiness, decay. There needed no explanation of the vanished pathway.

The Maori blood owns strange instincts. Again Vaiti knew what she was going to see before it came—knew, and walked straight over to a certain corner of the enclosure, as if she had been there before.... It was under a scarlet-flowered hibiscus tree that she found it—a long, low grave, fenced round with a wall of coral slabs, so that the overflowing bush had surged less thickly here, and one could see that there was something lying on the mound, only half hidden by creeping vines—something long and white and slender.

Vaiti dragged away the creepers.... Yes, it was a skeleton, bare and fleshless, with bony fingers and black, empty eyes. There was a splintered gap in one temple, and close to one of the hands lay a mass of rusted steel that had once been a revolver.

On a flat white stone, standing at the head of the grave, a long inscription had been carved with infinite care in three different languages. Two of them Vaiti did not understand, but the third was English. She pulled the growing ferns off the stone, and, wiping its surface, read:

> "Here is buried Junia, of the race of Vasilieff.
> Died 20th June, 1889.
>
> "Here is buried Anton, son of Junia Vasilieff
> and her husband, Alexis, Baron Varsovi,
> Born 20th June, died 21st June,
> 1889.
>
> "Here rests Alexis, Baron Varsovi. Into the
> unknown thou didst follow me: into the
> Great Unknown I follow thee.
> Reunited 21st June, 1889."

Vaiti, descendant of cannibal chiefs and lawless soldiers, more than half a pirate herself, and hard of nature as a beautiful flinty coral flower, was yet at bottom a woman after all. What passed in the breast of this dark, wild daughter of the southern seas, as she stood above the strange, sad record of loves and lives unknown, cannot be told. But in a little while, with some dim recollection of the long-ago, gentle, pious days of her convent school, she knelt down beside tie lonely grave, and, crossing herself, said something as near to a prayer as she could remember. Then, still kneeling, she cut and tied two sticks into the form of a cross, and set them upright in the earth of the mound. The sun was slanting low and red across the grave as she turned away.

\* \* \* \* \*

"What'd she give you?" asked Harris eagerly, as the bo'sun stepped across the gang-plank on to the quay. The lights of San Francisco were blazing all about, the cars roared past, there was a piano-organ jangling joyously at the corner.

"Fifty dollars for the two of us," said Gray, his acid face sweetened with unwonted smiles.

"Crikey! Honest men is riz in the market at last! What in h—— can she have got herself?"

"Might as well arst me what she got it for. Don't know, and don't care, so long as we've got the makings of a spree like this out of it. I see her comin' out of the Rooshian Consulate this mornin' lookin' like as if some one 'ad been standin' treat to her."

"You know she don't touch anything."

"I'm speaking figuryative; she looked that sort of way. And coming' back to the ship, she says to the old man, she says: 'Why, dad, better dead than alive!' she says. And he laughs."

"Don't sound 'olesome," observed Harris thoughtfully.

"Now, don't you get to thinkin', for you ain't built that way, and you'll do yourself a mischief," said the boatswain warningly. "And let's be thankful to 'eaven for all its mercies, say I, that we've got such a nice, warm, dry, convenient night for to go and get drunk in."

# CHAPTER X

## WHAT CAME OF THE PARIS DRESS

The effects of Saxon's illness in Fiji were a long time in wearing off. It was many weeks after Vaiti had come back to the *Sybil*, flushed with importance and with the lionising she had received on the cable-ship—many weeks after the voyage to the unknown island and the visit to San Francisco—that he took ill again; not very seriously, but badly enough to prevent his going to sea. Of course, the time was an awkward one. They were off Niué, and there was copra waiting to be taken to Raratonga for the steamer—copra which would certainly be secured by some other schooner if Saxon did not take it at the promised date. Neither Harris nor Gray knew enough to be trusted with the ship, and he did not much care about letting Vaiti sail her—not because he doubted his fiery daughter's ability or desire, but because, rash as he was himself at times, he knew her to be still worse. He had seen her run the *Sybil* in the trough of the very last swell alongside a barrier reef for miles, sailing all the time so close to the wind that the shifting of a single point would have meant destruction. He had heard her raving about the deck in half a gale as they swept up to the iron-bound coast of Niué, abusing Harris in the strongest of beach talk because he had not another main topsail in the locker to replace the two that had just carried away one after the other and battered themselves to ribbons—the principal ground of her complaint being apparently the fact that she considered herself labouring under a social disadvantage of the most mortifying kind because the schooner was obliged to come up to Niué for the very first time without all sails set. He had seen her perform tricks of steering, getting in and out of Avarua in Raratonga (a perfect death-trap of a port at times, as all old islanders know), that "fairly gave him the jim-jams," to use his own phraseology.... No, on the whole he thought he would rather miss that fright than lie idle in the trader's house at Avatele, and think daily and nightly of the cranky though light-heeled *Sybil* out upon the high seas in Vaiti's sole command.

This being so, it was natural and inevitable that Vaiti should set her heart upon going and carry out her desire. She did not make any trouble about the matter; neither was she at all unkind to the invalided owner of the ship. On the contrary, she paid the trader's wife more than that kindly woman wanted, to take good care of her father while she should be away, bought him everything decent to eat that the island contained (which was saying very little), indulgently presented him with a demijohn of whisky, and then informed him, in the coolest manner in the world, that the copra was all loaded, the stores and water on board, and the schooner ready to sail next day, under her command.

Saxon swore at large first of all, then stormed at Vaiti, and finally began a pathetic lament over his own helpless position and the heartlessness of his only child. Vaiti, sitting cross-legged on the end of his bed, smoked a big cigar through it all and looked out of the window. When he stopped at last, fairly run out, she laughed and handed him a weed out of her own case and a match.

"You take'm that, no speak nonsense. You know me, what?" she demanded; and Saxon, who was not in reality nearly as ill as he thought himself, laughed, and allowed himself to be won over.

Having gained her point, Vaiti went off again to the schooner through the wonderful pink dusk that wraps a South Sea island at sunset, and left the captain to hold commune with his demijohn and sleep.

As she walked down to the shore, she heard a sound of laughing and the rustle of many dresses among the palms close at hand. Now in Niué it is an important matter that brings people out of evenings, because, although the island has been Christianised long ago, like all the rest of the Eastern Pacific, it still suffers from a perfect plague of heathen ghosts that no amount of Sunday church-goings and week-day pious exercises seem to affect in the least. So the natives are afraid to go out of their houses after sunset, lest uncanny things should rise out of the forest to spring upon the wayfarer's back unseen and choke him. This Vaiti knew, so she suspected something of interest in the little crowd, and turned aside to look. If she had not, there had been no story to tell about Niué and the happenings there.

She saw a curious scene, so nearly hidden by the growing dark that no one but an island resident could have taken in its full significance. A group of islanders, men and women stood round the door of a big white concrete house with a pandanus roof—the finest native house in the village. They seemed to be waiting for something—something both amusing and exciting, to judge by the explosions of giggles that continually burst through the dusk.

Presently the door of the house swung open with considerable violence, and a large mat was thrown out by an invisible hand. Then the door was slammed, and the giggles redoubled. Within the house now sounded something very like a struggle. There were loud sobs and cries of a shrill, theatrical kind, scuffling, banging, and a dragging sound.

"Tck, tck, tck," went the tongues of the outsiders delightedly. The interesting moment was at hand.

It came without warning. The door burst open with still more violence than before, and out upon the mat was shot by some invisible agency a very solid young woman in a white loose gown, weeping somewhat mechanically, but with much effect. She fairly rolled over with the force of the shock that had ejected her, and before she could pick herself up the door was closed once more with a slam that shook the whole house. Then the waiting group rushed upon her with cries of joy, and bore her away in their midst, singing as they went.

"A wedding," said Vaiti to herself. "It must be Mata's; that is their house. And it will be a big wedding, too. I did not know that it was to be so soon."

She fell into a fit of musing as she wandered shorewards among the leaning palms.... The palms of Niué sweep downwards to the gleaming sea like a band of lovely maidens hurrying with sweet impatience to meet their lovers on the coral shore. Of a moonlight night, when all things are possible, and nothing seems too wonderful in an air that itself is wonder, it needs but little for those white, slender stems, and tossing, plumy crowns, poised high above the shadowy beach they curve to meet, to change themselves into South Sea dryads of a new and lovely race, and rush down, at long last, upon the calling sea, where Tangaroa, the king of ocean, has his dwelling. Under the palms of Niué, when the blazing white moon has risen so high in the heavens that a perfect star of jetty shadow is rayed about the base of every tree—when the wandering sea winds are held close by the breathless spell of midnight and nothing wakes on all the lonely shore but the long, long song of the droning coral reef—under the wonderful palms of Niué, loveliest and strangest of all the islands in that dreamy world of "perilous seas and fairylands forlorn"— nothing is too strange to be true, no fancy too wild to hold, when the moon is up and the palms are alone with the sea....

Was Vaiti thinking of visionary palm-maidens and sea-foam kings as she went down the winding path to the bay, through a wondrous afterglow of russet-rose laced through with opal moonrays? Perhaps—or of kindred fancies. I who knew her cannot say, for no one ever knew her altogether. It is more likely, however, that less poetic thoughts were in her mind just then. The scene she had witnessed in the palm-grove was the usual ceremony that takes place in Niué the night before a wedding, when the friends of the bridegroom come to the house of the bride's parents, and the latter go through the symbolical form of casting her out and closing the door, so that the bridegroom's people may take her over and guard her until the wedding morning. Vaiti liked a wedding above all things (next to a funeral), and the hint of great doings on the morrow, offered by the ceremony she had witnessed, decided her to stay another day. Why not? The copra was loaded, and no rivals were in sight. Besides, she had a motive for staying—the strongest possible motive. She wanted to wear her Paris dress.

Yes, it had been acquired at last. That day in San Francisco, when she had come out of the Russian Consulate with more money in her pocket than any one of her adventures had ever brought before, she had been able to restrain herself no longer. And thereafter, in Madame Retaillaud's elegant and exclusive Parisian emporium, replete with the choicest imported wares (I quote the lady's own description of her goods), there took place a scene that is remembered to the present day by those of Madame Retaillaud's young ladies who survived the earthquake year.

Vaiti, dressed in one of her waistless muslin gowns, with a broad-leafed island hat on her head, a long-bladed sheath-knife stuck quite visibly in the breast of her dress, and her wavy hair falling loose over her shoulders, stalked into the shop among the smartly-gowned San Francisco ladies who were turning over Madame's stock, and demanded to see—

"One dress belong Palisi, pretty dam quick."

They are used to all sorts of strange nationalities along the water-front in San Francisco, but not, as a rule, in the milliners' and modistes' well-bred establishments. Vaiti concentrated the whole attention of the place upon herself at a single stroke. She did not care about that in the least, but Madame's hesitation stung her, and she pulled out a thick wad of notes.

"Look 'em alive, my hearties!" she ordered impatiently in her quarter-deck voice. "Lay aft here with that goods. I want um Palisi model, all sort."

The customers were nearly in hysterics by this time, and the assistants were all a-giggle. Madame herself, however, grasped the situation in a twinkling, and frowned down the girls. Whoever and whatever this pirate queen might be, she certainly had money, and Madame would have welcomed Lucrezia Borgia or the Witch of Endor, under like circumstances, as pleasantly as an Anglo-American duchess.

"Perhaps Madame will come into a private room. Madame would like, no doubt, to look at our most exclusive goods, and we do not bring them into the outer shop," she said in her most honeyed voice. And the door of the lift closed upon the pair.

What Vaiti underwent in that fitting-room in the course of getting into Madame's latest model promenade gown, built for a typical French figure, will never be told. Early in the proceedings a message came down to the showroom for the strongest pair of Paris corsets in stock, and a little later Madame herself, very red and overheated, ran down to select a fresh silk lace.

"Ah, but she has courage, that one!" she declared, as the lift received her again. "Never, no, never!—jamais de la vie! ..."

The lift went up.

It was almost an hour before a wonderful vision sailed slowly through the show-room and out into the street—slowly, not alone for pride, but also because it could scarcely move or draw its breath. The vision, as described in the receipted bill that went with it, was made up of the following elements:

"One promenade costume (model, Doucet & Cie.) composed of chiffon velours, couleur poussière de roses, inlet with motifs of point d'Alençon, hand-embroidered with lilies of the valley in French paste. Mounted on chiffon bleu-de-ciel, with full volants edged lace and chiffon ruching. Made over foundation of glacé silk, couleur citron d'or.

"One set silk underclothing to match.

"One Corset Ecraseur, patent laces.

"One pair bronze promenade shoes, Louis XV. heels, extra height. Stockings to match.

"One parasol composed peau-de-soie rose fanée and chiffon bleu-de-ciel."

To which may be added—one young woman, suffering horrible agony and quite intoxicated with happiness.

\*　　\*　　\*　　\*　　\*

It was this marvellous possession that Vaiti yearned to show off at the wedding. She had not had a chance to wear it since the day when she had walked through the streets of San Francisco, with an admiring and amused crowd at her rear, and found it quite impossible to get on board the schooner, when she reached the water front, until she took off her voluminous skirt and handed it up over the side—afterwards climbing the rope-ladder in a storm of applause and a pink silk petticoat. Now the occasion for getting full value out of the wonderful thing had come at last, and she could not—no, she really could not—miss it.

Rather late next morning, when the bride and bridegroom—the former in a gorgeous gown of yellow curtain muslin, the latter in a thick tweed suit from Auckland that caused him to stream at every pore—were sitting on opposite sides of the little white church, enthroned on chairs all by themselves, and listening decorously to a long preliminary address from the native pastor— Vaiti swept in, and at once brought the ceremony to a momentary pause. The pastor stopped in his address and gaped, the women exclaimed audibly, the bridegroom fixed his eyes on the apparition and sighed in a manner that the bride evidently resented as a personal slight, for she grew still darker in the face than nature had made her, and stared penknives and scissors at Vaiti. Wild titters of delight swept indecorously through the church. The entry was indeed a success—the native pastor found it necessary to address his flock directly, and to tell them that they would undoubtedly all go to hell if they did not behave better in church, before order was restored.

It is not necessary to relate at length how Mata and Ivi were made one, how they walked out of the church nonchalantly by different doors, and were subsequently so deeply interested in the killing of the pigs for the marriage feast, and the preparing of the various cooking-pots, that they did not meet again all afternoon. It was a commonplace wedding enough, and this history is not interested in it, other than as it concerned the affairs of Vaiti. These, indeed, were fairly notable.

For with Vaiti pride very literally brought about a fall that day.

She had had a terrible time getting into her dress, and the whole ship's company had shared in the trouble. First, the native A.B.'s had to fetch her a big looking-glass from the nearest trader's, and secure it to the bulkhead of her cabin. Then the cook had to deliver up all the hot water in the galley— at seven bells, with dinner just coming on!—and the boatswain must needs broach the cargo for some special scented soap. Matters were only beginning, however. When the dress was disinterred from its many wrappings and finally put on it became immediately apparent that the bodice could not possibly be made to meet. Perhaps the coming of the bread-fruit season had caused the young lady's waist to expand—perhaps the practised art of Madame Retaillaud had exceeded anything that a mere amateur could compass in the way of lacing. At any rate, it was not till Vaiti had passed her corset laces out through the port and ordered two of the strongest sailors to tail on to them— not till Harris, agonising with laughter, had directed this novel evolution from the poop for at least five delirious minutes, during which Vaiti several times thought she was dying, but remained none the less determined to die rather than give in, that the deed was accomplished at last, and the "Kapitani" of *Sybil* was enabled to look at herself in the glass and know heavenly certainty that she was the best dressed woman in the Pacific at that instant, whoever saw or did not see.

The natural result of all this was that in the very hour of her triumph she fainted dead away in the church, for the first time in her life, and had to be carried out.

The ceremony was just over by now, and the bride, still burning with jealousy of the woman who had dared to eclipse her on her wedding day, was among the first of those who crowded round like bees going after honey, to stare at the beautiful creature lying senseless on the sunburnt grass. The bridegroom had sped away hot-foot in the direction of the village, whence certain enticing yells indicated that the pig-slaughter was now going on; but Mata was not a bit appeased by his indifference to the visitor. That dress—and oh, how wonderful it was!—still rankled in her soul.

Mata was a teacher's daughter, and she knew something of white people's lore. A brilliant thought darted into her mind as she pressed and struggled in the crowd about the deathly form on the grass....

"Ai, ai! she is surely dead!" wailed the people. "Ai! the-great chieftainess will rise no more!"

"Daughters of a turtle!" said Mata contemptuously. "I will show you if she is dead. It is nothing at all but that she is vain, and wanted to make herself a middle like the 'papalangi' women, who all look like stinging hornets. Give me a knife, someone."

A knife was given, and Mata, with horrid joy, half lifted Vaiti and slipped the keen point into the back of the dress.

Rip went the silk with a hideous splitting noise, and the delicate underwear swelled out through the opening like a bush lily bursting its sheath. Mata felt for the stay-lace, and cut that too. The tension on the bodice increased frightfully—the seams gaped and strained....

"She will die, I think, if I do not cut it off," said Mata hastily, feeling Vaiti reviving under her hand, and anxious to finish her work. Two more cuts of the knife did it. The Paris dress was, speaking sartorially, no more; the owner, lying on the ground, was opening her eyes to the outrage that had been done; and Mata, shrieking with malign laughter, was fleeing wildly through the palms in the direction of the pig-killing, peace in her heart again.

Peace was very far indeed from Vaiti's heart when she revived and found out what had been done. The crowd drew away from her in fear when they saw her flashing eyes and set, furious mouth, though she said never a word. Confronted by that Medusa-head, they were almost too terrified to find words; but one or two stammered out a hasty explanation that freed the present company from blame by inculpating Mata.

Vaiti did not doubt it—she had seen the bride's face during the ceremony. Still silent, but flashing looks of sheet-lightning all about her, she drew together her garments as best she could, and walked off in the direction of the ship. As she did so, a little ugly man with red hair slipped out from behind the trees, and looked narrowly at her retreating figure.

"It is the white man from the bush!" cried the girls. "White man of ours, why did you not come down for the wedding?"

"Because I didn't, my little dears," replied the newcomer in English, still looking after Vaiti. He stood well in the shade, and did not make himself unnecessarily conspicuous.

"That's a fine girl, that Mata," he added by and by. "A smart girl. I should like to know Mata."

Vaiti put off her going for yet another day. She had business to attend to.

It was very simple business, and it was characterised by the directness that attended all the proceedings of Saxon's daughter. She merely went up to the bride's new home, that was so handsomely stocked with trade goods and imported furniture, while the wedding party were making merry in the village after dark, and set fire to it with a torch in about a dozen places. It was very dry weather, and there was a strong wind.

There was scarce a stick of the cottage left when she marched into the village with a blazing torch in her hand, and calmly told the assembled revellers what she had done. Then she left them, seething in a tumult of excitement that almost drowned the hysteric screams of Mata, and went to bed and to sleep with a quiet mind, ready for an early start next morning.

The men came on board late and very drunk, but they did come. They were afraid of Vaiti, and so was Harris, who would very well have liked to extend his revels in the village for another twelve hours, but did not dare to do so. He thought, as he stumbled into his bunk, that the sounds proceeding from the forecastle were a good deal odder than usual—he could almost have sworn that there was one person, if not several, crying in there. But he had good reason for mistrusting the evidence of his senses just then, so he flung himself down and went to sleep.

# CHAPTER XI

## A DEAD MAN'S REVENGE

When one is well on the right side of five-and-twenty, with a good ship underfoot, a fair breeze setting steadily from the right quarter, and a pleasant goal ahead, it is hard to be unhappy. Vaiti's sense of bereavement at the loss of her cherished dress faded considerably before the *Sybil* had fairly cleared the land, and was gone altogether by the next day. She had done what she felt to be the right thing by Mata; the score was even. Vaiti did not like loose ends of any kind, and she had not left any behind her. She smiled as she thought of it, and paused in her official-looking walk across and across the poop, to revile a native A.B. for leaving the end of a halyard trailing on deck.

"You d—— lazy nigger," she said. "What sort ship you thinking you stop? You thinking one mud scow" (*Mud cow* was her pronunciation), "one pig-boat, one canoe belong dam man-eating Solomon boy? I teaching you some other thing pretty quick. Suppose you no flemish-coil that halyard, keep him coil all-a-time, I let 'em daylight inside that black hide belong you, knock 'em two ugly eye into one."

She plucked a belaying-pin out of the rail and sent it flying at the sailor's ear. Vaiti was a straight thrower, but the crew seldom failed to dodge; they had every opportunity of becoming proficient. On this occasion, however, the sailor made not the least attempt to escape, and the pin struck him fair and square at the angle of the jaw, and knocked him over. He was hurt, but not stunned, and sat up immediately on the deck, gazing at the tall white figure on the poop with lack-lustre eyes that scarcely seemed to comprehend what they saw.

"Bring 'em that pin," commanded Vaiti, still in what stood for English with her. She never addressed the crew in the tongue that was native to both.

The man crept slowly aft, and handed it to her. She motioned to him to replace it neatly in the rail, and then pointed to the trailing halyard. It did not escape her, as the sailor made his way down to the main deck, that there were tears in his large black eyes, and that his pareo was tied with a carelessness unusual among Polynesians, and significant of trouble and depression when seen. But she put the one down to the swelled and reddening bruise that marked all one side of his face and the other to the orgies of the previous night. If the men chose to make brutes of themselves on bush-beer, they need not expect that she was going to slacken their work for them on that account. No, not if she broke the head of every man in the ship. She was not Saxon's daughter for nothing, as they very well knew.

It was small wonder that Vaiti was not popular with crews.

She went on pacing the deck, in the joyous crystal-clear sunlight of the sea. The trade wind ran through the sky like a warm, blue river, the rigging sang, the sails drew steadily. It was a good day, a happy day, a pleasant day to be alive. The girl felt pleased with the world. She took the wheel from the sailor who held it, for the sheer pleasure of feeling the flying vessel answer to the touch of her own light hand. All the force and fury of those roaring sails overhead seemed to concentrate itself here in her fingers, as the power of a great dynamo passes through a single wire. It was almost as if she drove the ship herself. The *Sybil* went as steady as an albatross; once or twice the spokes fairly shook in her hands.

"The wheel is laughing to-day," she said in Maori, using the island sailor's expression.

Dinner-time came round soon, and she descended to eat with Harris alone. Saxon himself did not particularly care whether he dined with his bo'sun or not, if it happened to be convenient to leave Harris on deck; but Vaiti would have run the ship as strictly as a man-of-war at all times, if she could have had her way. Indeed, she would have liked to dine in solitary state, like the captain of a cruiser, had she not had too much good sense to fly in the face of merchant service custom by excluding the mate.

As things were, she graciously condescended to order Harris down to the cabin with her, and they discussed together the inevitable curried tin of Pacific cookery. It was wonderfully light and bright in the little cabin, which was large for the size of the ship, and had plenty of berth and locker space, besides its neatly fitted trade shelves. The bulkheads were painted white picked out with blue (they were satinwood and bird's-eye maple underneath the paint, a thing which had astonished and perplexed more than one ship's carpenter in the past quarter of a century), and there was a pretty bird's-nest fern in a basket hanging from the skylight, and the seats were covered with the neatest thing in blue and white trade prints that Auckland could produce. Vaiti's taste was evident everywhere, and Vaiti herself, hair freshly combed and held back with a bright ribbon, laces and frills dainty and immaculate as ever, looked, as she demurely poured out tea (you will seldom find the teapot absent from the table of a colonial ship), quite the last sort of person by whom a native A.B. might expect to be knocked into the scuppers. Yet, truth to tell, the unlicked Harris, wolfing his food at the opposite side of the table, was very much better liked by the crew, even though he was heavy-handed enough at times; and he certainly understood more about the five A.B.'s and one ordinary seaman who inhabited the forecastle than did Vaiti, who was half one of themselves, and therefore thought them beneath consideration as a rule.

Of this fact he proceeded to give an illustration when the curry and the tea and the fried bananas were almost done, and nobody's dinner could be spoilt by unpleasant news.

"Think you're in for a good time, don't you, Cap?" he said.

Vaiti, the economical of words, merely nodded. But her face spoke for her.

Harris was never quite sure whether he liked Vaiti in an uncomfortable, indefinite way, or heartily hated her. To-day the balance perhaps inclined in the latter direction. He watched her face with some interest as he said:

"That's where you spoils yourself, Cap. You ain't. And if you want my advice, which you never do, I'd tell you that the sooner you 'bouts ship and back to Niué the better."

Vaiti bit slowly through the piece of bread she was eating and deliberately chewed it, eyeing the mate all the time, before she condescended to answer.

"Mph!" was all she said at last. She had never studied diplomacy, but she knew how much more you learn in general by letting the other person lead the conversation than by talking yourself. And it occurred to her that Harris wanted to make himself important by hinting and patronising over some ship business which might, or might not, be in his department. Well, let him. She would not give him a lead.

Harris, on his part, got angry at once, and blurted out what he had meant to keep a good deal longer.

"Oh, very well," he said. "You can do just as you likes, of course, but where you'll find yourself when it comes to a question of mutiny, that's another two-and-six. Musling curtains on the ports, and white table-cloths, and ropes all flemish-coiled on deck is going to help you a lot then, ain't they? And if ever I've seen signs of trouble in a crew, I seen them to-day, and you knows it—ma'am."

The last word came with a jerk, screwed out, as it were, by an ominous flash of Vaiti's eye.

Vaiti herself was thinking very quickly indeed, but you would not have imagined it if you had seen her slowly scooping out the inside of a mummy-apple, and as slowly eating it. She was obliged to acknowledge to herself, now Harris had spoken, that there had been something unusual about the demeanour of more than one of the men since their departure yesterday. But mutiny? Nonsense! Indigestion from too much pork, more likely. She did not believe for an instant that any crew once handled by her father and herself would have an ounce of mutiny left in the lot, if you ran them through a stamp-mill and assayed the result three times over.

So she merely remarked, between spoonfuls:

"You talk plenty nonsense. You keep those men work, they no squeak. Suppose you finish eat, you go tell Gray he come down ki-ki."

"All right!" said Harris meaningly, trying to make an effective and tragic exit. He was really not at all easy in his mind, and Vaiti's attitude did nothing to relieve his apprehension of what might be about to follow. The men had never dragged on the rein as they had done these two days past, and he felt it in his bones that there was more than met the eye in the matter.

Vaiti, for her part, was so much incensed by the tone of his remonstrance that she would not even listen to the conviction which began to force itself upon her own mind, next day, that there was really something astray. Luck in general seemed to have deserted them. With a fair wind the schooner should have made the run to Raratonga in three days, but on the afternoon of the second day a dead calm had fallen, and they lay helpless in the trough of the sea by four o'clock, three hundred miles from anywhere.

"All-a-time I saying no good trust those trade winds, when that (adjective) Cook Islands be near," sighed Vaiti, scanning the horizon vainly right and left. Like a true sailor, she was generally cross in a calm.

"I wish we was out of this, ma'am, I do," remarked Gray, who was busy spinning sinnet at her feet on the deck. For some odd reason, the sour old bo'sun generally found her more approachable than the others.

"Why?" asked Vaiti, almost amiably.

"Because, ma'am, of that, for one thing. And hothers."

He pointed forward, and Vaiti saw what she had not noticed before, the ship's carpenter, a powerful young Mangaian, lying flat on the foc'sle head and obviously weeping.

"They've been at that game, one and another, off and on, ma'am, all to-day," he said. "And you know yourself 'ow we've been put to it to get the work out of them. Darned if I knows what monkey tricks they's up to, but I allow we're liable to understand all about it before very long, for that sea-lawyer of a fellow, Shalli, he's bin speechifyin' down in the foc'sle 'alf of this watch, like a bloomin' 'Yde Park sosherlist, he has."

Vaiti glanced at her watch.

"Make him eight bell," she ordered, scanning the foc'sle hatch.

"Ay, ay, ma'am," said Gray readily, passing on the order.

The watch below were prompt enough about turning out, but Shalli the forlorn could not, it seemed, find energy enough to get up and turn in.

Instead, he beat his curly head upon the planks and began to sob. Vaiti took no notice of him whatever, but just strolled nonchalantly for a minute into her cabin, and reappeared with a slight projection in the bosom of her muslin dress that had not been there before. Harris and Gray looked at each other significantly, and the former cast a swift glance about the vacant horizon. No, not a shred of sail, not a trail of smoke. Only the glancing flying-fish, and the oily, glittering swell, and the hard, pale, empty sky.

The men, who had all been standing in a bunch by the hatch, now signalled to Shalli, who put off the rest of his weeping to a more convenient season, and got upon his feet. Then the six began advancing slowly and uncertainly to the break of the poop. They were a good-looking crew in their way, all Eastern Pacific men, with bright eyes and well-featured brown faces, and their dress—the brilliant red or yellow "pareo" of the islands, gaily figured with enormous white flowers, and the bright cotton shirt or coloured jersey—lent a distinctly operatic air to the little scene. Vaiti and her officers, however (like Molière's *bourgeois* who had talked prose all his life without knowing it), had lived in the midst of picturesque and extraordinary things most of their lives, and therefore took no interest, as a rule, in anything save the sternest practicalities.

And it was stern enough in all conscience, this fact with which they were confronted. The men were mutinous, beyond doubt.

Vaiti's mind rapidly ran over all possible causes for the trouble, even while Shalli was stepping forward and opening his mouth to speak. It could not be rough treatment, because, as a matter of fact, the men were no worse handled on the *Sybil* than on most other island schooners, and an occasional knock-down blow is not the sort of thing that a Pacific native will seriously resent. It could not be any objection to go to Raratonga—the crew were mostly Cook Islanders themselves, and glad of a chance of seeing their homes. Nor could it be dislike to her command, for a chief rank counts tremendously among Polynesians; and islanders who were ruled at home by a queen of her family would be most unlikely to strike against the authority of one of the Makea race, unless for some very grave cause. It was, of course, possible that they had planned to seize the schooner and run off with it.... She put her hand up to her bosom, and played with the laces that lay over that hard substance under the dress....

But Shalli was speaking now, in answer to her sharp query as to what they wanted there.

He had a good deal to say, and he said it with flashing eyes and much eloquence, using his slender, pointed, brown fingers a good deal to emphasise his remarks, and turning dramatically from his mates to Vaiti, and back to his mates again. Harris listened anxiously, catching only a stray word here and there, for his knowledge of Maori was confined to the few phrases used in running the ship. Shalli was certainly saying that somebody was going to die—that somebody had got to die, and immediately—to judge by the emphasis with which he spoke.... The mate was, as Vaiti had once told him, rather chicken-hearted underneath his great bulk and strength. He felt himself turning chilly, for all the burning sky. What the devil did that fiend of a Vaiti mean by standing there listening as calmly as if they were paying her compliments on her eyes? Perhaps there was no particular trouble after all; but her demeanour was no guarantee, for she would have looked like that if they had all been on the verge of drowning, or burning, or hanging together, any day of the week.

Gray, on the other hand, did not trouble to try and make out anything, but cut a large quid and chewed it at leisure, idly looking on. He did not know if the men meant mutiny or not, and he did not particularly care. They were three whites against six niggers, and there were firearms on their side. And he had seen mutinies in his time beside which any little amusement that could be got up by half a dozen amiable Cook Islanders would seem a mere Sunday-school tea-party. Let them mutiny if they liked. It would not mean the interruption of the work for half a watch.

And Shalli went on talking as if he never would stop, and the *Sybil* rolled ceaselessly on the idle swell, and the useless sails slapped rhythmically upon the mast. And Vaiti, standing on the poop above the group of men on the main-deck, listened with an unmoved countenance until quite the end of Shalli's long speech.

When he had finished he turned his face away, and instantly began to weep. And the five other men, exactly as if a tap had been turned on, also began to weep at the same moment, howling loudly and lifting their hands to heaven.

"If this isn't a bloomin' mutiny, it's a bloomin' lunatic asylum," declared Harris quite inaudibly in the midst of the hideous noise from the main-deck. It is not a common thing, even in that world where all things are possible, the wide, strange Pacific Ocean, to see a whole ship's company shedding tears in concert on a calm and peaceful afternoon, with nothing more alarming in sight than a handsome young woman in an expensively pretty frock.

"Ow-ow-ow!" went Shalli, getting quite beyond his own control.

"Ey-ah, eyah!" screamed a plump lad from Aitutaki, fluttering his hands like frantic pigeons.

"For God's sake, Vaiti, tell us what's up," called Harris, sending his bull-like tones through the confusion.

And then Vaiti spoke, shrieking at the top of her voice in order to be heard. Her face, its hard calm broken up at last, was black with rage, and she had pulled out her revolver, and was holding it in her hand, though, strange to say, none of the men took the least notice of it.

"That ——, —— witch-man belong Niué, he curse them, they say they die!" she screamed. "By'n-by I cut him liver out!"

"What witch-man?" bellowed Harris. "Don't understand. That white bloke—him with the red hair and the scar on his nose—who dresses native, and lives native up in the bush? Saw him lookin' at you like as if he'd like to knife you, from behind Mata's house."

"No, pig-head! no white man got 'mana' for make die that way," shrieked Vaiti, shaking her revolver without effect at the men. "Niué witch-man. What man you mean? I not see——"

But she did see at that moment, and to Harris's utter dismay she dropped the revolver on the deck and flung her skirt over her head.

"My Gord! she's mad now," cried Harris. The crew paid not the least attention, but continued to weep with lungs of brass. The mate's head went round. He felt as if he was going out of his senses, too. Gray, who seemed to be the only normal person left on board, went up to Vaiti and plucked her dress off her face.

"Now, ma'am, keep 'er 'ead to wind," he remonstrated. "What's got 'old of the Capting? Blest if we ever saw you afraid before."

Vaiti turned on him like a tigress.

"You think me frighten, you parrot-face, bal'-head, humpback pig-monkey! Think some more those thing, and I shoot some hole in you lie-making tongue, learn you talk to me. I tell you——"

The hubbub on deck was calming down a little now, and subsiding into lost and homeless wails. It was possible to make oneself heard.

"I tell you, that thing Alliti see 'long Niué, he one dead man. Captain schooner *Ikurangi*—same I making tart [chart] all wrong, so he go drown, he and him mate. You think it good thing one dead man he go walk along Niué, looking me?"

"A cat may look at a king," said Harris, who had realised that no fighting was afoot, and therefore was very brave just now. "Besides, that red-head man wasn't no ghost—he borrowed a pouchful of tobacco off of me, and never paid it back."

"What sort that man?" demanded Vaiti. "He small, all same Gray, he ugly all same you, got red hair, cut 'long him nose, tooth all break?"

"That's him," agreed Harris.

Vaiti took a turn across the deck, and fell silent, angrily chewing a lock of her hair. The horrid vision of Donahue risen from his ocean grave, and wandering about the islands as a malignant ghost, bent on avenging his death, had struck her as such a fancy could only strike an islander, and almost paralysed her active mind. Now she realised that it was merely a case of mistaken newspaper report, and that Donahue had somehow escaped from the wreck of his schooner, and was once more roaming the islands in the flesh—at the very lowest ebb of fortune, it was evident, but probably none the less dangerous for that. She was quite certain that he was in some way at the bottom of this business of cursing the crew, although no doubt the witch-doctor and Mata had been intermediary. And it was no trifle. Sheer mutiny she would have much preferred.

"Wot's it all about?" asked Gray, who had not been so long in the islands as the mate. "Wot's the odds if a lot of bally niggers thinks they've been cursed? Seems to me anythin' the witch-doctor could do wouldn't be likely to harm a crew that's been salted by our old man in the cursin' way. There ain't no witch-what-d'ye-call-'em about the islands that can lay over 'im for language."

"Oh, shut up! You don't know anything about it," said Harris with irritation.

"Suppose you tells me," suggested Gray, tucking another quid into his cheek, and looking dispassionately at the crew, who were now lying on deck rolling about with the motion of the vessel, and looking half dead already. "Doesn't seem as if we was goin' to have much bother with that lot.... And you gettin' as white at the gills as a flounder, thinkin' they was goin' to take charge. Go 'ome and learn a ladies' dancin'-class, Mr. 'Arris; you ain't fit to 'andle men."

"I'll handle you if——" Harris was beginning roughly, when Vaiti, whose temper had been badly ruffled by the events of the last half-hour, stepped across the deck and delivered two stinging blows, one on Harris's right ear and one on Gray's left.

"You take'm that," she said. "Alliti, you speak bo'sun about Maori 'mana.' Glay, you lemember Alliti mate, no give cheek."

"Want to know if I've got any left for myself, before I start givin' it away," observed the bo'sun ruefully, rubbing his face. "But better be slapped nor neglected by a pretty girl, hany day, says I."

Vaiti did not smile, but leaned over the rail, and began staring at the crew. She was in no mood for flattery.

"Well, if you want to know, it's like this," said Harris. "These native blokes, they thinks some of their chiefs has got what they call 'mana.'"

"Wot's that mean?"

"Pretty near any thin', take it by and large, but one meanin's all we want, and that's the notion they have that these chiefs can sort of blast 'em with a curse, so's they'll go away and die. Like as if I was a chief, and you was a common man, same as you are, anyhow, and I was to say, 'Gray, you go off out of this and die next Thursday at four bells in the afternoon watch.' And you says to me, says you, 'Ay, ay, sir,' says you."

"Blowed if I would," ejaculated the bo'sun.

"Yes, you would, you chump, because you'd be a bloomin' native, and they always does. So off you'd go, and when Thursday come you'd lie down and die at four bells, wherever you happened to be."

"Wot of?"

"Nothin'—you'd run down like a watch—sort of 'stop short never to go again' business, like the grandfather's clock—and when you was dead you'd stay dead. That's all."

"And I never 'eard worse rot in all me days," said the bo'sun disgustedly. "Think I'm going to believe all that?"

"Who cares what you believes or what you don't?" demanded Harris, "You'll —— well see all about it soon enough. Vaiti she says they says Mata went to the witch-doctor, who they're as much afraid of as any chief in Niué, for all they're by way of bein' Christian, and he cursed them up and down and inside and out, worst style, and says they're all to die by sunset, to-night. And if I knows anything of natives they'll do it. I'll lay you, we got to work the ship up to Raratonga ourselves—if we ever get there. Of all the low-down, mean skinks that ever walked, them natives are the worst. They haven't a blessed scrap of consideration in them for anyone but themselves. Here we are with every man-jack of these fellows got an advance on his wages, and they says they're going to die! Die! I've no patience with them. I do hate selfishness and meanness."

# CHAPTER XII

## BREAKING THE MANA

Vaiti all this time had been steadily watching the men as they lay about on the main-deck in various attitudes of limp resignation. One or two—notably the emotional Shalli—were already beginning to look ill. Matters looked badly enough for the *Sybil*. It was in the hurricane season, and signs were not wanting the calm would break up with energy when it did break. If the crew persisted in their dying, other people who had not been in any way subjected to the witch-doctor's operations might find it incumbent on them to die too. She did not for a moment doubt the Niuéan's power to slay. Had she not more than once seen the queen, who was her own cousin, politely dismiss some offender with the significant remark, "I wish I may never see you again after to-morrow" (for the queen was always courteous, and would never have used the crude terms of a Niuéan witch-doctor); and had not every one on the island known that with the next evening's sunset the wretch would lay him down and die as surely as the dark would fall? These men were doomed, and the ship would miss the steamer and the cargo would not be sold, and possibly the schooner would be lost in the blow that was creeping up, and none of them would ever go home any more.

Thus the native side of Vaiti spoke. But now the white side woke up and demanded its innings too. Was it endurable that the red-headed rat of a Donahue (for she was as certain that he had been at the bottom of the matter as only a woman with no direct evidence to go on can be) should win the last move in the deadly game they had been playing this year and more. Was she to get into difficulties, and perhaps lose the ship, the very first time that she had taken off the *Sybil* all alone? The fact that such a disaster would include the losing of herself did not trouble, as it did not console, her. She would leave her reputation behind her, and people, when they spoke of Vaiti of the Islands, would say——

No, they wouldn't, and they shouldn't. The white blood was up now. It was impossible to prevent the "mana" from working. Well, let it be. She would do the impossible. She had done the impossible before, in many ways; it was the only sort of thing really very well worth doing, in the opinion of Vaiti of the Islands.

Whatever was to be done must be done quickly. The storm was not far away, and the *Sybil* was rolling in the trough of the increasing swell with every rag of sail set.

"What you goin' to do?" asked Harris hopelessly, as he saw her move. "Give them medicine? It ain't any good."

"Yes, give 'em medicine—you and Gray, you giving it plenty by'n-by," said Vaiti calmly, beckoning the two men over to her. The crew continued to lie on the deck, giving no sign of life but an occasional groan. The wind was beginning to cry a little among the rigging, just whimpering, like a chidden child. A glassy tinkling of foam sounded about the keel. The sun was almost down.

"You listen me," said the girl, her handsome, hawk-like features looking curiously sombre in the orange light. "I speak those men in Maori. I tell them some thing—thing not belong 'papalangi.' You no understan'. Wait."

Then, with a look on her face that the white men had never seen there before, and were never to see again, she stepped swiftly down the ladder, crossed the main-deck, and stood in the midst of the prostrate crew.

As though struck themselves by a spell, Harris and Gray remained motionless on the poop, only swaying with the unconscious movement of the sailor to the roll of his ship, while they watched with fascinated eyes the scene upon the lower deck. The crew at first lay still as logs, while Vaiti stood and looked at them—only looked. Presently they began to open their eyes and roll over, and the weeping, which had apparently ceased, began again.

Then Vaiti, suddenly flinging her arms high above her head, with her light muslin dress fluttering in the wind and all her magnificent hair falling to her knees, burst into such a flood of speech as made the two hard-bitten Englishmen on the poop open eyes of stolid amaze. There is no language in the world so full of eloquent possibilities as the Maori tongue—even in the somewhat debased and altered type that is current among the islands. And, hidden away somewhere in the strange nature of this strange thing in woman's shape, there was more than a touch of the true witch wildness and fire.

"Lord!" said Harris, in a tone of awe. "She's the devil himself!"

She looked it, as she stood there in that livid light, her arms stretched high to heaven, her voice—was there ever a voice so full of passion, prophecy, command?—ringing out, now high, now low, now in tones vibrating with some subtle suggestion of horror that caused even the uncomprehending whites upon the poop to feel a cold shudder about the region of the spine. Upon the crew the effect was marvellous, yet, from Gray's and Harris's point of view, unsatisfactory as well. The limp figures sat up, it was true, wept afresh, and even rose to their feet before long; but it was only to rush wildly up and down the heaving deck, driven, it seemed, by the sting of an agony greater than any they had suffered yet. Above the loose sails thundered and the wind wailed wickedly.

Gray, at a motion from the mate, went to the idle wheel and grasped the spokes. The *Sybil* would want watching soon.

"Strike me pink if this isn't the craziest ship's company outside a lunertic asylum from Yokohama to the 'Orn," muttered the bo'sun to himself. "Now, what the 'ell is *that*? Ho, Jemmy Gray, why don't you look for a berth as a bally stoker in a bally Red Sea liner, or a supercargo on a Chinese pirate junk, and 'ave a quiet life at your age? Here, Mr. 'Arris, you going to let 'er shoot 'erself before your heyes?"

Vaiti had plucked out her revolver again, but instead of threatening the crew with it, she was holding it close to her own curly head, all the time pouring forth a river of eloquent Maori, strongly charged with adjurations and threats. It needed no translation to understand so much, not to see the abject if inexplicable terror of the crew, who cowered and howled in an extremity of distress every time she raised the pistol to her head.

"Vaiti, Vaiti! What're you doing, Cap?" yelled Harris. "You'll shoot yourself! Are you crazy? What are you givin' 'em, for Cord's sake?"

Vaiti turned round, and cried angrily at him:

"Hold 'm tongue! You no leave me myself, very quick I shooting you. I tell those men I great chief, no one can take 'um curse away, but can come 'long all those men myself, suppose they die—go Raratonga when 'um night come, an' all those man soul he running quick, quick, all a-cold, 'long those mountains top Raratonga where 'um dead man he go to jumping-off place. A—a—h! I put one bullet in head belong me, very quick, suppose those men they got dam cheek go an' die. I coming, very dead, very angry, I go 'long that soul, all a-time; no let 'um rest, no let 'um see woman fliend, die long time ago—I take big club belong chief, make 'um run, cry, all-a-time—no sleep, no eat, no lie down! A—a—h! no go heaven, no go hell, all-a-time, for ever'n ever, Amen. I pay him out for going die!"

She stormed through the brief speech like a hot-season squall, and instantly returned to the natives. Harris, struck dumb by the entirely unprecedented nature of the situation, could find no vent for his feelings save in plucking off his cap and casting it under his feet. She was threatening the crew that she would kill herself if they died; follow them to the land of shades (the entrance to which was popularly supposed to be over the edge of a certain desolate, far-up mountain precipice in Raratonga), and make it so hot for them in the "otherwhere" that they would certainly wish they hadn't dared to die.... What on earth was a man to do in a ship commanded by a thing—he could not call it a woman—that talked like that—with night coming on, too, and something very like a bad blow unpleasantly near?

Vaiti did not leave him long in doubt as to what he was to do. The crew, driven previously to the verge of frenzy by her gruesome threats, became entirely frantic during the eloquent peroration that followed her address to Harris. They ran up and down the deck; they shrieked, they prayed, they besought. Vaiti, with the eye of a hunter watching a quarry almost driven to bay, kept a keen look-out through all her fiery eloquence, and just at the moment when the men seamed driven to the highest point of human endurance, turned to the mate with a triumphant cry.

"Now, Alliti! he all right by'n-by: I no shoot myself, I think. You and bo'sun you get rope's end very quick, give 'um order shorten sail, make 'um go. I think he go; he too much plenty frighten die 'long me."

"Too much plenty frighten" the men were indeed. The threat that Vaiti had made—for the carrying out of which they doubted neither her ability nor her will, any more than she did herself—was so much more potent than the curse of the witch-doctor that the terror of the one paled before the terror of the other. For the moment, they felt that they might not be able to live, but they certainly must not die; and it was right in the middle of this illogical state of mind that the mate and bo'sun came in with their rope's ends and settled the matter once for all. An hour ago, red-hot irons only would have moved them to hurry up with their dying. Now a couple of ropes' ends, laid about among the six with a will, drove them howling up the masts and out along the yards, where, with Gray and Harris still after them, and Vaiti threatening from below, they succeeded in getting the sails stowed and the vessel snug in very little over the ordinary time. The blow that followed kept all hands busy the night through, but it came from the right quarter, and the *Sybil* fled before it at such a speed that morning found her only half a day's run from Raratonga, with the wind quieting down to a pleasant breeze, the schooner uninjured, and the crew as cheerful and busy as they had ever been in their lives.

Vaiti caught the steamer, sold her copra, and saw it on the wharf ready to load. Then she went back to the schooner, and waited till the last of the men returned.

"Suppose you like go die now, plenty time for you," she said. "Plenty good sailor-man stop Raratonga. You go 'long die; I no want."

The men looked at her sheepishly, and Shalli, the spokesman, scratched his head and surveyed a heap of tributary pigs, fowls, and fruit that lay on the deck of the schooner before he answered. The crew had many relations about Raratonga, and the relations had done them very well this trip.

"Many thanks, great chieftainess," he said at last, in his own tongue. "We are much obliged to you, but we have changed our minds, and now we do not ever mean to die at all."

# CHAPTER XIII

## THE GAME PLAYED OUT

Every one in the trader's had gone to bed, and Vaiti, barefoot and dressed in dark cotton, had just got out of her room by the window, and was gliding noiselessly down the back verandah.

The moon was down, and the thick darkness under the trees of the village covered her safely as she slipped along at the backs of the little white, palm-thatched houses. It was not at all likely that any native would be about in the middle of the night, but one could never reckon on white men, of whom there were several in the little town—and Vaiti, being engaged as usual on "urgent private affairs," did not want any inquiries.

She got away from the village without remark, and then struck into one of the narrow grass roads penetrating the bush. Everything was asleep. The little green parrots were hidden deep under heavy leaves, each with its noisy head tucked under its wing. The lizards that had been darting and flickering all day long about the path now slept, chill as little stones, among the roots of the trees. There was a cold, dewy smell in the air, and the palm-tree plumes were motionless as drawings in Indian ink against the violet gloom of the sky. Very far away the immemorial music of the reef beat softly in the dark.

Vaiti girded her dress high, and walked swiftly. She had a long way to go, and she wanted to be back in her neat, white, mosquito-curtained bed, sleeping the sleep of the innocent, before the trader's wife should come in with her morning cup of tea. Vaiti was a past mistress in the art of avoiding useless comment.

Three miles, five miles, seven miles.... It was right at the other side of the island, past mile after mile of tangled bush, acre after acre of sparsely planted, rocky, open ground, grove after grove of tall, plumy cocoanut, heavy with fruit. Oranges grew by the track here and there; broad green banners of banana leaf blotted out whole sections of the stars, and slim, quaint mummy-apple trees stood up among the prickly coral rocks. Vaiti had no time to stop, but she snatched a little refreshment on her way from time to time, as the wayfarer may always do in the kindly South Sea climate.

She struck at last into a narrow track leading off the main pathway—so small that in the dusk of the starry night it must have been invisible save for a mass of pointed rocks that stood up just beside the overgrown entrance and made a landmark. Afterwards came a mile or two of tangled walking among clumps of pink and scarlet and yellow hibiscus, all reduced to a common blackness by the levelling night, and through thorny lemon-trees, and over rocky knolls where there was scarce footing for a goat.... A lonely God-forsaken region this; not a village, nor even the gleam of a solitary white-washed hut. What had the "Kapitani" of the *Sybil* to do with such a place?

Vaiti knew very well indeed what she had to do. She had gathered in the town that the mysterious white man who "lived native" in the bush had his dwelling about this lonely neighbourhood. It was very well known to her, and she meant to find the man's dwelling-place, and see him with her own eyes before....

Well, that was still to come.

It took her rather longer than she had expected, but she did at last succeed in finding the tumble-down little palm-leaf shanty, built against the side of a rock, that she had heard described. It was a miserable place, so far as her cat-like eyes could judge it in the purple gloom, not more than three or four yards long, and looking like nothing so much as a heap of dead leaves and rubbish piled against the rock. She trod noiselessly round its three sides, and listened here and there. The door, as she ascertained by feeling, was a heavy mat hung up from the eaves, and it was tightly fastened across the opening. There was a faint sound of slow, heavy breathing from within. The man was evidently asleep.

Vaiti climbed up on the rock above the hut, and pulled away a piece of the loose grey coral of which it was composed. Then, sheltering herself behind a clump of hibiscus growing in a cleft, she raised her voice in a fearful squealing cry, exactly reproducing the yell of a wild pig wandering in the bush at night. At the same time she cast a lump of coral with all her strength down the side of the big rock, whence it landed with a crash in the middle of a mass of brushwood, burying itself completely.

The double noise, as she had anticipated, brought out the owner of the hut, very cross and sleepy, clad only in a pareo, and angrily anxious for the safety of his patch of yams. He carried a torch in his hand, made of blazing candlenuts strung on a stick ("Must have run out every bit of credit at the stores," thought Vaiti parenthetically), and he was, beyond all shadow of doubt, against all common probability, the red-haired master of the *Ikurangi*.

If looks could ever blast, those black eyes behind the hibiscus boughs would have slain him where he stood. Vaiti quivered with rage as she watched him shambling sleepily about, looking, with his long, matted red hair, bloated, evil face, and half naked body, infinitely lower than any coloured native on the island.... He had not prospered since he escaped the wreck of the *Ikurangi*— how or where she did not care to know. He looked as if he had been living on the natives and half drinking himself to death, as was indeed the case.

But Vaiti was not in the least mollified by his unprosperous case. In her opinion, he ought to have been dead long ago. There could be no peace of mind for her while he was still drifting about the Pacific, ever on the alert to do her an evil turn. She was not equal to actual murder, and, in any case, Niué was a British-owned island, with a resident Commissioner and a regular nest of missionaries, where you had to be very careful of what you did. But if any accident—a safe, convenient accident—should befall him by-and-by, why, it would certainly be an advantage to the *Sybil* and her owners. Well, that might come about, and without introducing Saxon into it either. In such a delicate matter Saxon's interference would very likely have acted much as a charge of dynamite might act in the destruction of a wasps' nest—something more than the wasps would probably come to grief.

She waited until the ugly creature had rolled back into his cottage and shut the make-shift door. Then she slipped down from the rock once more, and began the second part of her errand. Neither then, nor at any other time, did she trouble to find out the manner of Donahue's escape. If she had, she would have heard that he had been picked up by a native canoe, floating about on a piece of wreck the day after the disaster that destroyed the *Ikurangi*, and that, he had spent a good many months on a neighbouring island before a stray schooner had consented to accept his watch for passage money and convey him as far as Niué—the only place near their course where a penniless beachcomber would have been allowed to land. As things were, he was more or less smuggled off, and thought best to take refuge in the bush at once. The moneyless adventurer is not encouraged in islands belonging to the British Crown.

It is easy, therefore, to understand why Donahue, living under an assumed name in the far interior of the island, had not been recognised, and was not likely to be, by any one save the person whom his presence most concerned. His malice against Vaiti had by no means evaporated with the events that took place on Vaka. He did not, as it happened, suspect her of having actually caused the loss of the *Ikurangi*, but he was of a darkly superstitious nature, and laid down his ill-luck, first, last, and all through, to the fact of her influence. She had been a "Jonah" of the worst kind to him, and he would have been very glad indeed to serve her any ill turn of any kind that might be possible. But only the small piece of spite compassed through Mata had, so far, lain within his power.

Vaiti had still a mile or two to go, and it was waxing very late, or rather, early. She almost ran along the winding rocky path, following it as easily as if broad day or full moon had surrounded her instead of star-lit dark. Now the sound of the sea, unheard for the last hour, broke out again, and a cold salt breath from the beach cut through the heavy perfume of the forest track. In another minute she was out of the wood and fairly running down a sloping, sandy track that led to a little white house standing alone on the shore.... She laughed as she ran—it was such a soft, clear night, and the sea called so pleasantly down in the dark, and she did so dearly love an adventure—especially when all the world imagined her to be sleeping quietly in her mosquito-netted bed.

There was no secrecy about this matter apparently. The house had a good wooden door, and she rapped loudly on it with a stone, calling at the same time, "Sona! Sona! Wake up!"

There was a brief interval, in which the rollers tore at the beach and the palms swung and crashed overhead, uninterrupted by other sound. Sona was evidently asleep. She struck loudly on the door again. This time some one answered in a drowsy voice, and a slow, shuffling foot came to the door. The hinges creaked, and in another minute a small, bent, feeble figure appeared on the threshold.

"Tck! tck!" it clucked. "Is there magic in the air, and have I grown fifty years younger, that the lovely maidens come to my door in the starlight once more? Is it my beauty that has struck you to the heart, chieftainess Vaiti; or do you want a charm to catch the love of some one less deserving than myself?"

A fit of coughing interrupted him; he crept out to the open air, and clung to the door-post, shaking all over with the violence of the paroxysm. There was more light here, down by the foaming rollers; one could see, if one had been walking half the night in the dark bush, that the man was very small and hairy, very decrepit, and very, very old. Indeed, the personal appearance of Sona, solitary recluse of the Avarangi beach, good Nonconformist Christian on Sundays, and heathen witch-doctor out of business hours, was a very important item of his stock-in-trade. He looked his part to perfection, and knew it. His very name was a piece of business, even though, rightly pronounced and written, it was that of the godly man of Nineveh. When Shark-Tooth of Avarangi had consented, largely for reasons of policy, to join the mission fold a good many years before—the last straggling heathens on the island having been then "brought in" by the exertions of a determined and energetic missionary—he had selected the name of Jonah for his baptismal title solely because, so far as he could ascertain, the original bearer of the name was proverbial for bringing bad luck to his enemies—and that was the sort of reputation that Shark-Tooth especially coveted.

Vaiti had not met him before, but she knew him well by reputation, and was very sure that he knew all he cared to know—probably a good deal—about her. It was, she thought, a case for going straight to the point, so she went very straight indeed.

"Let me in, Sona," she said in his own tongue. "I want to talk with you, and I want to buy you; for you and I are wise people, and I know that there is nothing that may not be bought."

"Crah—crah—crah!" cackled Sona, in a feeble old man's laugh, tacking a joke to the end of it that might well have raised a blush on Vaiti's cheek if she had been capable of such a weakness. He led the way into the house, still cackling, lit an ill-smelling kerosene lamp, and sank down upon the mats, a mere heap of crumpled cotton clothes, old bones, and ancient wickedness.

Vaiti pulled out her cigar-case, tossed the old creature a cigar, which he clutched at eagerly, and lit one for herself. Then she squatted down on the mats, her back against the wall, and puffed for a minute or two in silence. Old Sona watched her eagerly with his glassy little eyes. He saw that she was not angry at the part he had played in the late unpleasant occurrence upon the schooner, or at least that she did not mean to resent it. He had heard all about the strange happenings of the voyage, and was a good deal awed at the power of the woman who had actually broken the spell of his curse—in which, be it observed, he believed most fully himself, with excellent reasons for doing so. And he was really very anxious to know what she wanted now, and especially what he was going to make by it.

Vaiti pulled at her cigar vigorously for a minute to make it draw well, and then, with a leisurely puff, remarked in Sona's own tongue:

"Mata gave you a gold ring to curse my sailors that they should die—all the village knows of it, so you need not deny it, old man with the face of a scavenger-crab. Was it not foolish of you to set yourself against Vaiti, the great sea-princess—very foolish to run into danger, and for so little?"

"Yes, yes, so little," repeated Sona, in a kind of wail.

"Now I come to buy you for myself," went on Vaiti, puffing between words (she smoked like most women, very hard and fast). "I buy like a great chief's daughter, and you shall feed and drink well for a long time if you are faithful to me. If not, I shall split you open with my knife as one splits open a fish on the beach, and leave you out on the strand, so that the crabs may come and eat you before you are dead. That is what I shall do to you."

"I belong to the high chieftainess, soul and liver," quavered Sona nervously. Vaiti, hardly looking at him, pulled something out of her dress and flung it down carelessly on the mat between the two. Sona's eyes glittered, for he heard the chink of gold.

"Take it, old pig of the woods," said Vaiti contemptuously, and he clutched eagerly at the little parcel of rag. It contained a roll of gold coins. Sona, panting with mingled delight and fear lest his visitor should change her mind, scuttled away to some hiding-hole in an inner room, and concealed the packet with breathless haste. Then he returned to the lamp-lit room, where Vaiti sat smoking and waiting.

"I am yours, high chieftainess; I am yours," he repeated, rubbing his hands together and cackling.

"What is this thing they tell about a devil that stays upon the road to Mua, and comes out at night-time?" asked Vaiti carelessly, looking over Sona's head at the wall.

Sona shut up his eyes very tight, and shook his shaggy little head from side to side.

"If you ask the good misinari doctor, he will tell you," he answered. "As for me, I have nothing to do with devils. I am a very old man, and I want to go to heaven.

"You will go to-night, old scorpion-head, if you do not tell me everything I want to know," remarked Vaiti. Her tone was pleasant, but there was a flavour of something else below the pleasantness that caused Sona, literally and figuratively, to sit up.

"I tell, I tell, high chieftainess," he stammered eagerly. "The thing is known to all the people on the island—even the white people. It happened only last year, and it is as true as the Good Book. It was the foolish man from Mua way, whom they called a witch-doctor—and every one knows that such a thing does not exist, high chieftainess; but they said he was that thing, and he said so himself, because he was proud and mad. Now, we all know that there are many devils on Niué, and that the misinaris never were able to drive them all away. And there is a very bad devil on that road to Mua, right where the six palm-trees stand up by themselves among the graves. It is powerless in the day, but at night there is no Niué man who would dare to go there. Sometimes the white traders will ride past the place coming home in the dark, but it is a true thing that their horses will often shy and bolt when they come near to the home of the devil, and no man can say why; indeed, the devils, for the most part, do not have power over the 'papalangi.'

"So this witch-doctor, as he called himself, said that he did not fear the devil, and he would go and stay the night among the graves, thinking that because of that all the people in the island would believe in him, and give him many pigs and yams for fear of his 'mana.' So he went to the devil-place, and all night he stayed, but in the morning he did not come back at all. And by-and-by all the people of his village went together to look for him. And they found him lying on the road, all dead, and his face was black and his body twisted up. So the people brought him to the misinari doctor, and he said that he could not make him alive again. And the traders said, 'What is the kind of this death? We do not know it, though we are white men and know everything.' But the misinari doctor did not know. And they buried him, and that is all, high chieftainess."

Vaiti smoked thoughtfully. She had heard something of the tale before, and Sona's story did not vary from the version that was generally current about the island. She thought, on the whole, that she believed in it. There was no doubt that many of the white people gave it credit, though a few of them declared the man must have died in a drunken fit. A paper in Australia had published an account of the mysterious incident, and the spiritualistic set in Sydney were so deeply interested in it that a letter of inquiry from a psychical research society had been sent up to the island, inquiring into the matter. But it happened that the trader to whom the letter was addressed had committed suicide a good many months earlier, and excellent onions and pumpkins (much appreciated by his successor) were growing green upon his grave by the time the letter reached the island. So the inquiry was never answered.

Yes, on the whole, Vaiti thought she believed the story. That a similar result would follow in the case of a "papalangi" (white man) who followed the deceased magician's example she did not, however, believe. She thought it very likely, however, that mischief of one kind or another would result.... And if the worst should chance to come about....

Vaiti took another cigar.

"What does your misinari say?" she asked. "He is not the right sort of misinari, it is true, but still, he should know more about devils than the traders."

"Our good misinari was not here when it happened," replied Sona in a pious tone. "It was the doctor misinari. Our own good misinari says that devils cannot do harm to any but bad men."

Vaiti reflected, her eyes on the floor. She really had some respect, in an odd, upside-down kind of way, for missionary opinion. It is bred in the bone with the younger generation of Eastern Pacific islanders.

Donahue was certainly a very bad man. She did not think she had ever met any one much worse. Perhaps the badness, balanced against the whiteness, might swing down the scale. At any rate....

"Hear me, Sona!" she said, in a voice of command. "I have bought you to-night, and you belong to me. There will be more to pay by-and-by if you do as I tell you. But I would warn you to be careful, for you will not find it pleasant lying on the shore down there, with your inside hanging out like a gutted fish, and the crabs coming running to eat you before you are dead, as you will if you make any mistakes. Listen, then, very carefully."

"I listen, I listen!" cried Sona.

# CHAPTER XIV

## HOW THE WITCH-DOCTOR GOT HIS MONEY BACK

When the trader's wife came in next morning with Vaiti's cup of tea, she was touched to see how deeply her pretty lodger was sleeping.

"Poor young dear," said the good woman, "lying there so sweet and innocent, sleeping like a baby! It's only the good heart that rests like that. I don't believe a word of the silly lies they tell about her. Here, dear, wake up," she called gently. "Your good papa is ever so much better this morning, and looking for you to come in. And it is Sunday morning, and a nice cool day."

"Thank you, Mrs. Smith," said Vaiti politely, broad awake at once. "May I asking you one little hot water? I like get up and go to turch."

Church, attended for reasons religious or otherwise, was not one of the amusements patronised by the nameless white man of the bush. Indeed, his amusements, such as they were, were so far confined to the native villages of the interior that very few of the other whites had seen him. He was not good for trade, having no money and possessing no credit—that was all they knew, or for the most part wanted to know, about him.

There was all the more astonishment, therefore, in the shanty owned by the Mua trader, away up in the bush, when the unknown man walked into the store that Sunday night, and demanded some tobacco, at the same time showing a sovereign he held in his hand. He was dressed in a pitiful mass of rags, none too clean, but he looked well pleased with himself, and was more than half drunk. Fortune had apparently found him out at last.

The Mua trader was an honest man, but he did not see why he should not have a share in anything good that happened to be available about that lonely and unprofitable district. So he welcomed the stranger in with much cordiality, and asked him to stop for supper.

The newcomer had no objection in the world to come in and share the trader's good tinned meats and new yeast bread, and he made himself very much at home without pressing. The trader, who had a private store of consolation in his own back kitchen, plied the spirits freely. He was curious, and he believed in the old saw of "Wine in, truth out." A couple of friends who had ridden over from Alofi, the capital, and were equally curious about the derelict's sudden access to fortune, did their disinterested best to help, and the bottle went merrily round. The Niué traders are a sober, decent set of people enough, but Donahue had mixed with them so little that he did not know this, and consequently was not put on his guard by the unusual conviviality. Indeed, he was by no means the same active, crafty villain who had set that successful snare of the diamond necklace in Apia many months ago. A white man cannot "live native" without going downhill very fast, and Donahue was nearly at the bottom.

So he drank, and laughed, and told evil tales, and grew quarrelsome, and pathetic, and finally affectionate and confidential, in well-defined stages, while all the time the other men kept sober, or nearly so. The Mua trader in particular hardly touched his glass. But Donahue, once so wary, never saw, and chattered on.

Before midnight the trader had sold him some gay calico for the native' girls, and a little tinned meat and flour, and half-a-dozen various trifles that brought the score up to about a pound. Here the guest came to a pause and fingered his coin.

"Oh, well, if that's all you have, you won't get any more goods to-night. Thanks," said the trader, putting out his hand.

The visitor, however, declined to hand over the money. He would pay to-morrow, he said. He was not going to leave himself without money again—not if he knew it—and he would have lots to-morrow: and if the trader wouldn't send up the goods without the cash to-night, why, he might keep his condemned rubbish, and his customer would go elsewhere.

Rather than lose the order, the other gave in, and sent a boy away with the stuff. It would always be easy to bully him out of it afterwards, he thought, and there was no arguing with a drunken man's whim.

Then he set himself, in company with all the rest, to find out where the money had come from.

Donahue, who by now was far gone, responded readily. It was the silly old chap who lived down on Avarangi beach, he said; an old fool who was an uncle of a girl who was a friend of his. The old chap had a notion that there were some Spanish doubloons hidden somewhere on the island, but in a place he was afraid to touch, so he had forked out a good British sovereign, and offered it to Donahue to go in his place, and share the money with him. Donahue was to keep the earnest money for his trouble, if nothing came of it, and if anything did turn up he was to take half. So he was going, that very night—the sooner the better. Natives were—well, natives; but as for him, he was afraid of nothing.

"Thasser-sort-er-man I am," he finished thickly, looking round for applause.

He did not get it. The traders one and all burst out laughing. The story of the doubloons, they told him, was a very old one in the island, and only the newest of new chums thought of believing it. It was quite true that the natives, who were perfect magpies for hoarding, did possess among them a certain number of doubloons, which came from God-knows-where—for the coinage used in the island was British—and true also that the trader would get a doubloon from one of them every now and then in the course of business, always with some mystery attached to it, and some reluctance to part with the coin. But the Resident Commissioner, who knew the island pretty well, and the missionary too, had long been certain that the store was merely the remains of some ship-wrecking raid of past days, about which the Niuéans were now ashamed to speak. They were great misers, and it would like enough be another generation before all the hoarded coins had come to light and passed through the traders' hands. But hidden treasure in Niué! Pf! If old Sona had been giving away money, he must be either going mad with age or (more likely) up to something. He was the cutest old fox on Niué, and that was saying something. Why, when he had come into that very store to buy a darning-needle a few hours ago (what a man who lived in a waist-cloth and nothing else wanted with a darning-needle he hadn't explained), it had been all the trader could do to prevent his picking up half-a-dozen odds and ends. That was what he was like if one ever took an eye off him; and he wouldn't even pay for the needle, either, till the trader had threatened to hammer him unless he forked out. Take his word for it, if Sona had been giving away money, he meant to have it back—somehow. And the treasure was poppy-cock.

Donahue had now passed into the quarrelsome stage, and he rose with tipsy dignity from his seat.

"I considdle you no gennlemen," he said scornfully. "For half a Chile dorrer I'd" ... He mentioned what he would do, in gross and in detail, to the assembled company for the small sum mentioned.

"Kick the dirty brute out," said the Alofi trader disgustedly. "It's easy to see what sort of company that carrion has kept."

Donahue was gone, however—gone with surprising agility, and lurching rapidly up the forest pathway towards his house. His legs were always the last thing to fail him.

He knew very well that he had had too much, and when he reached his hut he proceeded to sober himself by dipping his head repeatedly in a bucket of water. Then he brewed himself a powerful jorum of black tea, drank it, and set off considerably sobered.

It was a long way to the clump of palms, and he stumbled badly now and then as he went over the graves that lay thick about the edges of the path. Burial along the high-road is very popular in Niué, where they like to keep an eye on their dead and see that they are lying quiet in their graves—a thing that no one considers at all a matter of course. Some of the graves that Donahue passed had felt hats laid upon them; others had plates, bowls, bottles of hair-oil, fans—all to amuse the ghost and keep it quiet; and one or two looked ghostly enough to scare a nervous person as it was, with the wraith-like mosquito curtains thoughtfully suspended over the tomb by mourning and anxious relatives. Every grave was completed by a solid mass of concrete, weighing anything from several hundredweight to a ton. It was not the fault of any Niuéan if his dead relatives "walked."

Donahue as he went chuckled to himself at the thought of his keenness in over-reaching the old witch-doctor. He had used him for his own purposes through the girl Mata before, and though that had not worked out too well, it was the witch-doctor who bore the discredit, not he. He would use him again now, and in another way. It was in the daytime that Sona had arranged to meet him at the palm-tree clump. At night, he said, it would be certain death; and even in daylight no one would linger there who could help it. He at least would never dare to disturb the big tomb in which the money was hidden and call down the anger of the devils on himself, unless he had a white man with him who feared nothing. So next morning, very early, the white man who was so brave would meet him, and they would open the big, cracked tomb together—the tomb that no Niuéan had ever dared to lay a finger on before, though there were one or two besides himself who suspected that it was just there the mysterious foreign coins had come from years ago, and that there were a good many left.

Thus the witch-doctor. And Donahue had assented eagerly, and gone off with his earnest money. And, on arriving at his hut, he had looked out an old axe that he possessed, and cleaned up his lamp, and begged a drop of oil from the nearest native house. For he meant to go that very night, and take everything there was for himself. Who was to prove it?

Which was just the course of action that Sona had calculated very confidently on his taking.

It poured furiously in an hour or two, for it was in the hot season, and the great rains were out. Donahue could not light his lamp when he came to the clump of palms, which he knew well enough to recognise almost in the pitch dark. It thundered soon after, and the sky was split from pole to pole by corpse-blue flashes of lightning. In one of these, Donahue, feeling about the cracks of the tomb, thought he saw something moving against the gloom of the bush near at hand. It made his throat turn dry, for all the wet, and he felt his hair prickle curiously. But he went on groping. Another flash ripped up the sky; it was a smaller one, but for one horrible moment he thought he had been struck, for something stinging streaked across his face and gave him an ugly thrill. But it passed immediately, and he began groping again—groping with both hands, in a frantic hurry, trying to make out the best place to apply the axe—tearing and grasping and scuffling like some deadly graveyard mole, breathless, with beads of warm sweat coursing down his face through the streams of chilly rain.... He was fighting—fighting he knew not what and knew not why—but he was fighting, for all that, fighting hard, with the stone falling away from his nerveless hands, and the breath in his body sinking down under some nightmare oppression, and the sound of the thunder now almost continuous, blending itself with another and far louder sound that was battering madly in his ears. He was fighting with—— Christ!—it was Death!

The thunder passed, as tropic storms do pass, suddenly and completely. The dawn shot up in the east, wet and red, and cast long, black, ghostly shadows, set shaking by an icy wind, low down upon the palm-trunks and the grave. But Donahue did not want the light. The axe lay untouched beside him; and he lay over the tomb, dead. And his face was black and his body was all contorted.

It was barely daylight yet when something small and slow crept out of the bush, and began hunting carefully near the corpse. It could not find what it wanted, seemingly, and this distressed it, for it whimpered pitifully in a thin old voice, and looked long before it desisted. Then it put its claws into the dead man's pockets, and hunted through them, before it finally disappeared down the road.

*    *    *    *    *

The Mua trader was at his door when a howling procession of natives came into the village, carrying the white man's corpse to his home. The Alofi trader, who had found the body, stepped aside to speak. After the tale of the finding had been told, the Mua trader asked slowly:

"Did you think of searching his pockets? A dead man's a dead man—and I'd not be sorry to have the money he owed me, for the natives will have taken the goods by this time."

"They were empty when I found him. Queer, for I was the first to see him," said the other. "I found this thing on the road close by, though. Do you recognise it?"

It was the trader's darning-needle, stuck neatly into the end of a tiny, arrow-like reed, and stained at the point with some dark sticky stuff.

The Mua trader took it in his hand, smelt it and looked at it closely. Then he walked to his kitchen, and, watched by the Alofi trader, threw the thing into the fire.

"That's what I think of it," he said. "My boy, I traded in the worst of the Solomons for three years. I'm the only man on the island that knows that thing, bar one—and he was a plantation hand in the Solomons, in the black-birding days. There's no wanderers like the Nuié men."

"Do you think——" began the other.

"I think," said the Mua trader, "that old Sona has got his money back."

*    *    *    *    *

The schooner *Sybil* had no reason for staying longer in Niué, for the business of the ship was done, and the captain was quite well again. A picture of perfect beauty the *Sybil* made, as she stood out of Alofi roads in the golden afternoon, every sail set and every inch of cloth straining to the merry breeze. Niué was sorry to part with Vaiti, for she had interested the island considerably, and her beauty had, as usual, won her more admiration than her temper deserved. Every one, on parting, expressed a courteous wish to see the *Sybil* and her owners again.

For all that, and all that, the schooner came back no more. Vaiti had won the game at last, but she never willingly mentioned Niué again.

# CHAPTER XV

## THE CALAMITY OF CORAL BAY

The wide, still waters of Coral Bay were turning glassy pink under the sunset afterglow. The *Sybil's* boat, rowing rapidly towards the schooner, left as it went a long, ugly flaw upon the stainless crystal of the sea. It was very still, and the night was coming down.

Even in that uncertain twilight the colour of the boat as it cut through the pale-hued water stood out strange and sinister. Most boats are white in tropic seas: the *Sybil's* had always been snowy as her own graceful hull. Now they were vivid scarlet, and the ship herself had a wide band of scarlet round her counter and flew a scarlet flag at her masthead.

Any islander could have told you at a glance what these things meant. The schooner was "recruiting"—conveying natives from the wild cannibal islands of the New Hebrides to the Queensland sugar plantations. Ten pounds a head was paid for the men on their arrival, and it was politely supposed that these ignorant heathen had one and all been duly engaged under a contract to serve three years, at a wage of five pounds a year. How much they understood of contracts, times, and wages—where and what they thought Australia might be—and what were the means employed to get them on board the ship, nobody asked. Saxon was not the man to answer, if any one had.

Why he had temporarily deserted the pleasant, peaceful islands of the Eastern Pacific, and gone "black-birding" in the wild and wicked and fever-smitten groups of the West, was Saxon's own affair. Doubtless he had his reasons; possibly they were satisfactory. But there is reason to believe that about Apia and Papeëte at this time he was characterised as a (double-adjectived) liar, and an (impolite expression) villain, who was running away because it was (adverbially) unsafe for him to stay and risk his (past participled) neck among (adjective) men. This is not the history of Captain Saxon; at least, not all of it—from such a recital as that may the eleven thousand virgins of Saint Mudie, and the Blessed Young Person of Sixteen, deliver us! It must therefore be enough to say that, for sufficient reasons, he decided to shift his headquarters to the New Hebrides, and immediately did so, leaving behind him certain unsettled scores with which this tale has nothing to do.

He was not new to the islands or the natives, having been one of the most notorious of the sandal-wood traders in years gone by. The sandal-wood was gone, and of the money he had made by it not even the memory remained. But there was still something in the labour trade, and Saxon liked the lawless atmosphere of the place.

Vaiti remembered the islands well, though she had only been there as a child, and she was glad to have the excitement of the change. When the recruiting boat left the schooner (guarded by a companion, full of armed men) and drew up on the beach to negotiate with the islanders, she always sat in the stern, with a very smart little Winchester rifle across her knees, and took command, if her father was not there. Very often he was not; for the New Hebrideans have long memories, and there was many a spot where Saxon had run up so many bad, black scores in the sandal-wood days that he could not hope for success—or safety, if he had minded that—in going ashore. Harris usually took command of the covering boat, a post of comparative security that suited him very well, while the dauntless Vaiti managed all the real business, and seldom came back with an empty bag.

They had good luck, on the whole, and not many narrow escapes. Coasting round the notorious island of Mallicolo, or Malekula, they succeeded in obtaining about forty natives in a week or two. Saxon was well pleased, and began to count up his profits. Also he began to drink again.

Then it was that trouble came, as trouble generally does, out of a fair-seeming sky.

Half-a-dozen natives had been given up to the missionaries on the far side of Malekula, to hand over to the British gunboat *Alligator*, which at that time was cruising about the islands, intent on punishing the Malekulans for a more than usually atrocious murder of whites. The tribes to whom the culprits belonged had taken fright, and were anxious to save themselves at any cost. The missionaries, when asked by them, consented to take charge of the prisoners, but refused to keep them any longer than could possibly be helped, since they did not consider themselves judges or gaolers. At this point the *Sybil* turned up, and the missionaries, hearing she was bound for Parrot Harbour, where the *Alligator* was certain to call, put the men on board, and engaged Saxon to hand them over to the Parrot Harbour mission, receiving from the missionaries there the price of their passage, which the man-of-war would doubtless refund.

Saxon, understanding that he had not to meet the *Alligator*, undertook the job at a rather excessive rate, and brought the prisoners over as agreed. But, finding that the Parrot Harbour mission refused to pay the passage money until the man-of-war arrived, he went into a towering rage and abused everybody. Wait for the *Alligator*? Not he! He had something else to do, and he wouldn't have any condemned gunboat that ever sailed the sanguinary waters of the Pacific poking her nose into any of his business. He had been promised the money as soon as he arrived, and the money or its equivalent he meant to have or know the reason why. Off he went, with much more whisky in his brain than was compatible with sober judgment—off out to sea again, taking with him the whole six prisoners, and openly declaring his intention either to hold them for ransom or run them down to the Queensland plantations, as seemed most convenient.

Next day the *Alligator* appeared, and her commander was informed of the occurrence. Saxon, master of a miserable labour schooner, had run off with prisoners of war belonging to a British gunboat, defied the Imperial Government, and offered open disrespect to the Crown! The commander, an iron-faced, flinty-eyed disciplinarian of the toughest school, and a first-class pepper-pot into the bargain, nearly choked with rage and indignation. Out went the *Alligator* again, full steam ahead, making the captain's dainty suite of cabins tremble like an ill-set jelly in the stern as the ship forged along at thirteen knots an hour, blackening the crystal sky with trails of smoke, and looking implacably about for the offending *Sybil*. That delinquent of the high seas was farther off than might have been supposed. The wind, though light, was in her favour, and she had managed to get round the far end of the island, and down the other side to Coral Bay, eighty miles off, before the *Alligator* came up with her, late in the afternoon. Once caught, her shrift was short. The prisoners were at once transferred; Saxon was arrested and taken, still half drunk, on board the man-of-war, and his ship was confiscated, "just to learn him," as Gray (who had viewed his captain's proceedings with sour and silent disapproval throughout) was heard to remark, not without a little I-told-you-so satisfaction.

And so it came about that Vaiti, returning with the boat from an unsuccessful recruiting expedition, and not in the best of humours to begin with, was met on her arrival with extremely unpleasant news.

"We're took, cap'n; we're took, ma'am!" shouted Gray over the bulwarks, as the boat nosed along the side of the schooner. He added a rapid account of the calamity, in which he was careful to suppress his personal feelings of triumph.

The smart young lieutenant who had been left in charge of the ship came and looked down at the boat. He wanted to know what sort of person it might be who was addressed with this extraordinary hail. He had been under the impression that the "captain" of the *Sybil* had been left two hours ago—sullen, swearing, and not at all sober—in the cells of H.M.S. *Alligator.*

What he saw was a red-painted boat, manned by four stalwart native seamen, and steered by an extremely handsome, olive-faced young woman, who looked up at him with eyes that seemed to dart black lightning under their beautifully drawn brows as she listened to the boatswain's story. She wore a dainty, lacy white muslin frock, and carried a Winchester rifle in her lap.

Second Lieutenant Tempest, who had been cursing his luck up to that moment, suddenly became reconciled to the uninteresting job in which he was engaged. It is just conceivable that his commander might have selected another officer to perform the duty if he had been aware of its possible alleviations; for Mr. Tempest was notoriously given to scrapes with a *soupçon* of petticoat in them, and had already imperilled his career more than once after this fashion. But Commander the Hon. Francis St. John Raleigh had not seen "Captain" Vaiti; so he sent Mr. Tempest to take possession of the *Sybil*, and slept the sleep of the well-conscienced and well-dined, that evening, in his velvet armchair.... It might have seemed somewhat less perfectly stuffed to him, had his dreams been concerned with what was happening a few hundred yards away.

Mr. Tempest, smiling like the godmother beast of his own ship, offered his hand to the sullen beauty as she swung herself up the *Sybil's* side. Vaiti tossed it indignantly away, favoured him with another black-lightning glance that reduced his susceptible sailor heart to pulp, and stalked aft like an offended Cleopatra. Tempest, persistently following, poured out explanations, apologies, smiles, consolations, promises. Vaiti began to think that civility might possibly avail her something, and began to melt by carefully calculated degrees. Before very long she was sitting on the main hatch, with Tempest beside her, holding her hand unreproved and continuing his consolations. The commander was very angry, no doubt, but he was a good sort at bottom, and perhaps he would not really seize the ship. She would be sent to Fiji, no doubt, and Saxon might possibly be imprisoned, but it would all come out all right, trust him! And he would take very good care of the *Sybil* and her charming "captain."

Vaiti, still smiling sweetly, dug her nails into wood of the hatch at her side. Underneath all this verbiage she foresaw the reality of serious trouble. Why had her father been such a fool? What could be done to save the ship? There seemed no way of helping Saxon himself. If the commander proved implacable, to prison he must go. Well, that would not break any bones; but the loss of the *Sybil*—if such a disaster was indeed possible—must be averted at any cost. She did not believe Mr. Tempest's smiling assertion. The commander had threatened to confiscate the ship, and most probably he would. At any rate, the risk was too great to face. The schooner must not be taken to Fiji.

The wily brain was hard at work, as she sat on the hatch, listening, with a gentle smile and soft, downcast, maidenly eyes, to Tempest's love-making, and answering now and then in her pretty Polynesian "pigeon-English"—so much simpler and less grotesque than the *bêche-de-mer* talk of the Melanesian Islands.... If he could be got out of the way, and the marines suddenly overpowered, the schooner might slip off round the corner of the headland in the dark, and get nearly a hundred miles away before daylight, with the steady wind that was blowing outside the glassy, landlocked harbour of Coral Bay. There was just enough air stirring at this farthest point to allow her to get out, and once off, she could show her heels in a way that would astonish even a British gunboat. Of course, the latter would easily overhaul her in an open chase, but Vaiti did not propose any such folly. There was many a perilous inlet and passage among those dangerous, ill-surveyed islands where the *Sybil* could safely go, but where the *Alligator* could not venture. Let them only gain a day, and who was to say whither they had flown into the wide wastes of the Pacific? Once beyond pursuit, paint and other disguises would so alter the ship that no one could identify her; her name could be changed, and the *Mary Ann* or the *Nautilus* would innocently sail the seas formerly polluted by the presence of the naughty *Sybil*.... It was certainly worth trying.

As for Tempest, she had a plan concocted to get rid of him almost as soon as the matter entered her mind. She left him, by and by, solacing himself with fresh turtle steak and excellent champagne in the cabin for the loss of his own dinner, while she went into the bows with Harris and Gray, and rapidly explained her plans. The marines had been accommodated with eatables and drinkables after their own hearts, on the cover of the main hatch, and were too much engaged to notice anything in the thick darkness that was now lying heavily on Coral Bay.

Vaiti's plan was simple and effective. Tempest was to be enticed into leaving his duty and going ashore—she would see to that. Four of the New Hebridean crew, stripped of their ship clothes, and attired in their aboriginal paint and plumes, were to be concealed on the beach. They would capture him, and carry him off to a bush village near the coast, where the people were not ill disposed to the whites, and leave him there, scared no doubt, but safe until the morning, when he would be let go. Vaiti would come back to the ship as soon as the capture was effected, and the four native sailors would hurry down from the village as quickly as possible. Meantime, it would be easy for Harris to drug the marines' drink and make them helpless. They would be set adrift in one of the boats, as soon as the schooner was clear of the land, so that they should tell no tales. With good luck, everything should be over, and the *Sybil* far out to sea, in less than a couple of hours.

\*   \*   \*   \*   \*

Of the disgrace of Lieutenant Tempest—of his temptation, his struggle, and his fall—there is no need to tell at length. The decline of a British officer from duty and honour—his desertion of a post which every professional instinct should have compelled him to keep is not a happy subject, as (fortunately) it is not a common one. Vaiti, in brief, invited the officer to leave the ship unguarded, and slip ashore with her, to sup at a neighbouring trader's shanty, where she said there would be drink and dancing, and every kind of fun. There was no such place, but Tempest did not know that; and if he had known, he might not have cared. Half-crazed with love and champagne, he thought only of the beautiful half-caste girl, and was ready to follow her to the mouth of hell, if she had asked him. The dinghy was got out softly and cautiously, and, with muffled oars, they slipped away unheard. So far out of his mind was the lieutenant that he did not even note the disappearance of his men, who were all lying, very ably and completely Shanghai'ed, in the hold.

In less than half an hour Vaiti came back, swimming the stretch of black water that lay between the *Sybil* and the shore, to leave the boat ready for the men. Dripping, sparkling, and laughing, she stood up in the dim light of the deck lantern and told the mate and boatswain how the capture had been managed. Tempest, with a sack over his head and his hands and feet bound to a pole, was at that moment being carried up in the dark to the bush village. The inhabitants of the place were to have ten pounds' worth of trade goods promised them to keep him there all night and let him escape in the morning, when they themselves would go off and hide in the impenetrable forests until the man-of-war had sailed away again. In half an hour or so the four natives would be back on board, and they would all sail away round the headland, and leave no evidence of any kind to connect the *Sybil* with this last unpardonable outrage; for Tempest could not but suppose that the natives who so neatly bagged him as he was philandering along the dark beach with the innocent Vaiti were ordinary hill tribesmen. And, in any case, his sacred person would be taken good care of.

"Then he ain't to be damaged, the little darlin'?" inquired Harris. The question was not an idle one. Every one on board the schooner knew that Vaiti was capable of ugly things at her worst.

The girl laughed—a low, gurgling laugh.

"No. No kill him, no hurt him. I not like," she said, tossing back her wet, wavy hair, with a coquettish gesture that told Harris the woman in Vaiti was fully awake that night, despite the rough and ready adventure on which she was engaged. Harris was no fool, if he was something unsteady in character, and more or less he admired Vaiti himself, which tended to sharpen his sight.

"Good job the dandy leftenant *is* out of the way," he growled as Vaiti disappeared into the cabin to change. "'Twouldn't take much for 'er to get fancyin' his silly face, after all, and then the fat would be in the fire."

"Well, if you hask me, I don't like none of the 'ole thing from beginnin' to hend," declared the bo'sun, jamming a wad of tobacco viciously into his pipe. "Not the keepin' of the bloomin' niggers, not again runnin' to Coral Bay, nor again this business. Wy? Because I don't, and because it make me smell dirty weather. Give us a light."

Overhead the stars in the velvet sky began to twinkle here and there as the breeze rose and the clouds melted away. An odour of hot, wet jungle drifted out across the bay from the invisible land, and a locust with a rattle exactly like a policeman's whistle burred loudly among the trees. It might have been half an hour, and it might have been more, before something else became audible—something that sounded like a frightened wailing on the shore.

"A—wé! A—a—wé!"

Vaiti came out of her cabin and stood on deck, listening intently.

The sound went on.

"A—wé! A—wé! A—wa—wé!"

Harris, watching Vaiti's face in the light of the lantern, saw it change and harden, but she said nothing. There was another sound now—a dinghy shoving off from the beach and the rattle of carelessly handled oars.

"What's the —— fools makin' such a —— row for?" asked Gray. "They'll 'ave the *Halligator* on to us."

Still Vaiti said nothing, but stood like a statue on the deck, listening and looking into the darkness.

The boat rammed the *Sybil* in another minute with a shock that made her quiver, and then drifted aimlessly along her sides. Three brown naked figures lifted up their arms from below, and cried despairingly:

"Kapitani! Kapitani! A—wé! A—wé!"

"Get those fellows on board, too much quick, and bring him cabin," ordered Vaiti. Harris and Gray hauled them in with small ceremony, and dumped them down the companion into the cabin, where they stood in the light of the lamp, painted, feather-bedecked creatures, fierce enough in appearance, but in reality abjectly frightened and a-shiver.

"What thing you been do?" demanded Vaiti sharply. "Where you make other sailor-man? What you do Tempesi?"

One of the men was beginning his wail again. She seized him by the shoulder, pulled a pistol from among her draperies, and shook it in his face. The man, with a yell of terror, twisted himself out of her hold. Harris, who was rather frightened at her demeanour, got him away, forced a dram of spirits into his mouth, and tried to extract the terrified creature's story from him by degrees.

# CHAPTER XVI

## THE FATE OF THE LIEUTENANT

It was not a gratifying tale. Half a mile from the beach, the captors had been overtaken by a party of wild hillmen from Ranaar, one of the worst of the inland cannibal towns, and had been set upon fiercely in the dark. Aki, one of their own party, had been clubbed, and his body carried off. The other natives had escaped. As for the lieutenant, the Ranaar men had seized on him with cries of joy, exclaiming that now indeed they had a chance of "making themselves strong" before all Malekula. Then they had carried him away, slung on a pole between two men, and the *Sybil's* people, half dead with fright, had run down to the beach again; and here they were, begging the Kapitani to have mercy on them, for indeed it was not their fault, and no one could have known that the Ranaar men would venture so near the coast.

Vaiti, Harris, and Gray all looked grave at this recital. They knew only too well what was implied by the phrase "making strong," and what virtues the hill tribes of Malekula ascribed to the eating of white man's flesh. The rude play of the capture had turned into most serious earnest, and Tempest's life was worth just so many hours as it might take the cannibals to reach their mountain stronghold and go through the preliminary ceremonies of the feast. No more.

There was silence for a minute or two, while the schooner rolled gently on the swell of the incoming tide, and the smoky kerosene light flickered to and fro upon the strange, wild scene: Vaiti's beautiful, angry head standing out above the weather-beaten faces of the two English sailors, the three naked New Hebrideans, squalid and monkey-faced, cowering before her; the remnants of Tempest's dinner, some one's greasy pack of cards, and a couple of Saxon's empty whisky bottles decorating the table. The natives were badly frightened still. They did not understand that the Kapitani's plans had been entangled beyond all hope of setting right by this disaster, or that the *Alligator* must have been alarmed by their noisy return; but Vaiti's countenance was enough to warn any one who had ever seen the unpleasant things that happened at times on board the *Sybil* that hurricane weather was ahead. But before she had time to speak again, a loud hail from outside made every one look towards the deck. In another moment the first lieutenant of the *Alligator* had framed his smart white and gold personality in the dark oblong of the companion, and demanded, loudly, and authoritatively, to know where Mr. Tempest was, where the marines were, and what the deuce was the meaning of all this.

Vaiti, motioning aside the mate and bo'sun, swept to the front and spoke straight out.

"All your sailor, he too much drunk, sleep 'long hold. Tempesi, he been go shore. Men belong Ranaar, they catch him, take him away. Pretty dam quick they eat him."

"Great Scott!" said the officer. Facts were falling very thick and fast, and there were evidently more facts behind them which for the present he felt obliged—most reluctantly—to neglect. People think quickly in the navy, and Lieutenant Darcy realised instantly that this strange, wild, handsome creature was speaking the truth, and that it must be acted on without delay.

He stepped out on deck, and gave certain orders to his men. A sharp little midshipman and half the boat's crew followed him on board, and planted themselves about the ship. The rest remained in the boat.

"This officer will stay here and take charge, and you will come with me to the *Alligator*," said the lieutenant, addressing Vaiti.

"Yes, I speak captain. Very good you let me see him quick," said the girl imperiously; and the lieutenant, guessing that there was more still to be told, hurried the boat away.

He delivered his report to the commander, and concluded by saying that the girl was in waiting, and had, in his opinion, something more to say about the matter.

"Bring her in," said the commander shortly. The gravity of the affair had darkened his face a trifle, but he made no comment. It was not a time for talk.

Vaiti entered with the light step and carriage of the woman who wears neither shoes nor stays, and stood silently before the commander, fixing his hard grey eyes with her inscrutable dark stare.

"You can sit down," said the officer. "I want to ask you some questions."

Vaiti drew herself up a little higher.

"No time for sit," she said curtly. "Suppose you no want Tempesi ki-ki [eaten] pretty quick, you listen me."

"Young woman!" began Commander the Hon. Francis St. John Raleigh sternly.

"I tell you, no time talk!" interrupted Vaiti. "I savvy all right you very big sea-chief; I savvy my father been made bad work, made bad work myself. Let him go all-a-same that; by-'n-by we talk those thing. Now you listen me."

"All right; sit down," said the officer in a more conciliatory tone. Vaiti sat, and leaning across the table with her chin in one slender hand, and her eyes blazing out from under the mass of damp waves on her forehead, she said her say.

"You no savvy Malekula man; I savvy plenty. Suppose you do what I telling you, Tempesi he come back, I think. Suppose not, Tempesi he eat. Ranaar, he ten, eleven mile up 'long bush, plenty bad way. You take some sailor; he go too much sof', too much quiet, all-a-same cat. Time we coming along Ranaar, one half-mile, sailor he all stop. I go myself Ranaar. Maybe I get Tempesi; we coming back to sailor, go home all right."

"Oh, nonsense! how are you going to get him, if the men can't?" demanded the commander. He saw that he had a remarkable personality to deal with in this strange half-caste beauty, but he did not comprehend her very clearly, and he thought she was "gassing" a little.

Vaiti frowned.

"I tell you, you no savvy Malekula," she said scornfully. "Sailor belong you, all the man hear him when he walk 'long bush. Ranaar man he hear; he run away."

"Well, so long as we rescue Mr. Tempest——"

"No you talk, I say; you listen, you Kapitani with um wooden face!" spat Vaiti.

The lieutenant turned his head away, and choked a little in his pocket-handkerchief. The commander stared, then burst out laughing.

"Go on, you she-cat," he said.

"Ranaar man he run away; very good. He leave Tempesi; very good. No want Tempesi tell some tale, so he leave him dead. Break him head, all same pig, very quick, then run away. Now what you think?"

"I think you are a very plucky young lady, and that you have something more to say about it," replied the commander politely.

"Very good. Suppose I going 'long bush; savvy plenty the way. I been 'long Ranaar recruit; savvy all-a-road. No walking all same white man, walking all same one snake, all same one mice. No white man he walk that way. I come up Ranaar, all-a-dark, I stop 'long one small place; see the man he dance, he sing, he make ki-ki. Bushman, he plenty frighten something he no savvy. Savvy gun, dynamite, but no savvy big blue-light signal thing you got 'long ship. I take one, two blue-light thing; I throw. Bushman he think one big devil stop, no think man-of-war come; run away too much dam quick, not stop kill Tempesi. By'n-by he coming back, but I cut rope before he come. I bring Tempesi 'long me, 'long sailor-man; we go back quick. Tempesi all right. Savvy?"

"Yes, I do savvy; seems a neat plan, on the whole. But what's going to happen to you if they catch you?"

"Eat," said Vaiti succinctly. "Now you listen me. I no do all this thing for nothing, see?"

"H'm; yes, I do see. How much do you want?"

"Two thing," said Vaiti, eyeing him narrowly. "One. My father say he plenty sorry, no do any more bad thing. You let him go, let schooner go."

"Well—yes, I'll promise that," answered the commander rather stiffly. The girl was taking her life in her hand to serve the interests of the British Crown, and it was not a time to stick at trifles, or, indeed, larger things.

"Two," went on Vaiti. "Tempesi he seen leave ship, go 'long shore with me. You tell him all right, you no punish."

"Oh, by Jove! that's too much," snapped out the commander. "No, Miss— Miss What's-your-name, I can't promise any such thing. I can't have you or any one else interfering with the discipline of my ship. Mr. Tempest's conduct is a very serious matter, and he must take the consequences, by Gad he must, if he comes back alive to take them."

Vaiti had had a good deal to do with men-of-war, and their officers, during the course of the schooner's many wanderings. She did not need to be told that Tempest's career might be ended, and his life disgraced, if naval justice took its course. A few hours ago she would not have cared. But Mr. Tempest, like all men notorious for getting into scrapes with a petticoat at the bottom of them, had a "way with him," and it happened to be a way that appealed to this daughter of the Islands more than she would have cared to allow. Besides, it was not her custom to give in to a defeat.

"All right," she said calmly. "I savvy all thing about Englis' officer. Tempesi he no like court-mars'al, make break, make longshoreman, all the people laugh. Tempesi, he like die, I think. All right. I let him. Good night."

The commander held out his hand.

"Good night," he said politely. "Mr. Darcy, you will see about getting a native guide who can show the way to Ranaar, at once. We will do our best to surprise them."

A low, sarcastic laugh came from Vaiti.

"You wooden-faced Kapitani, you think you savvy Malekula!" she said. "Where you get guide?"

Mr. Darcy did know a little about the New Hebrides, and he saw that they were beaten.

"She's right, sir," he said. "Take my word for it, no native would dare to guide you. There's no mission here; they're a very bad lot, and all at war."

It was a bitter moment for the commander, but he surrendered like a gentleman.

"You've got the best of me, Miss—Miss Saxon," he said. "Very well. You have my promise. Mr. Tempest shall be pardoned, if we get him back alive. You know nothing about this matter, you will remember, Mr. Darcy. Miss Saxon, you're a very brave young lady, and I wish I had met you in circumstances of which I could more honestly approve."

"No one need tell me," he said afterwards, "that that old vagabond we had in the cells wasn't a gentleman once. It comes out in the girl; blood will tell, even in a half-caste. But Providence ought rightly to have a down on the man who is responsible for any one of them, for there seems no right place for them, either in heaven or earth."

\*     \*     \*     \*     \*

Neither the bluejackets of the *Alligator*, nor the officer appointed to command the column, ever forgot that night's march through the mountain bush of Malekula. The air was like hot water, and not a breath of wind was stirring. The track was but a few inches wide, and as slippery as butter, so that the men slid and fell continually when struggling up the endless sides of the innumerable gullies. Mosquitoes settled in bloodthirsty hordes upon their faces and hands, roots tripped them up, saw-edged reeds slapped them in the eyes, and thorny tangles of bush-lawyers fished for and successfully hooked them. At any moment a huge soft-nosed bullet, cruel as a shell, might come singing out of the darkness; or a poisoned arrow, freighted with sure and agonising death, might whirr across their path. When the officer in command, irritated by the stumbling and falling of the men, ordered them to remove their boots and march barefoot, Vaiti told him that nothing of the kind must be done, for poisoned spear-heads were in all probability set here and there in unsuspected places, ready to pierce the unwary foot. She herself seemed invulnerable and untiring; she led the column at a pace that caused more than one to fall out, and never hesitated nor faltered through all the three hours of the worst and most intricate march that the *Alligator* men had ever known.

At last she told the officer to call a halt, and on no account to make the slightest noise or advance his men until he should see a blue light burning about half a mile ahead. Then she vanished into the darkness, lithe and noiseless as a lizard, and silence, dead and oppressive, settled down upon the bush.

\*     \*     \*     \*     \*

Lieutenant Tempest was a man and a British sailor, and he was not afraid of death. But he thought there might be pleasanter ways of dying than that which actually stared him in the face.

Memory plays strange tricks when the dark is closing down about her doors. Lying there on the damp earth, bound hand and foot to a pole, with the hideous howls of the cannibal dancers in his ears and the glare of the cooking-pits in his eyes. Tempest could think of nothing but a fragment of verse out of a half-forgotten poem read somewhere long ago:

"It isn't the fact that you're dead that counts.

But only—how did you die?"

How was he dying? Not as an English officer might gladly die in the cause of his country and in loyal obedience to orders. Not even as a man, with a sword in his hand, facing the foe. He was dying an unfaithful servant, false to his trust, and suffering because of that falseness, as a slaughtered brute struck down with a club like a bullock, and afterwards....

The red remains of the luckless Aki, jointed and piled in a ghastly heap, told the rest.

Tempest did not look at that ugly pile any more than he could help. He wanted all the nerve he could muster for he was haunted by a deadly fear that he might cry out for mercy when it came to the last, and he did not want to add cowardice to the tale of his many shortcomings. If he could have died here as a prisoner of war—as a captured scout, a fighting enemy, taken in a skirmish—the death, hideous as it was, would have been honourable, and his pride of country would have upheld him. But it seemed as if his courage had nothing to stand on now, and he was almost—almost, but, thank God! not quite—afraid.

The Malekulans had been dancing for full two hours, ever since they had brought him to the valley and flung him down upon the ground. In the middle of the open village square were three huge idols, carved out of entire tree-trunks set upright. They had black, empty sockets for eyes; their mouths were curved upwards into a ghastly wrinkled grin, and their tongues hung mockingly out. On the head of each was perched a huge black wooden bird, with beak bent down and gloomy wings outspread—the very spirit of Nightmare herself. Round and round these devilish things, in the red glow of the fires, danced the cannibals ceaselessly and untiringly, fleeing with heads down and outspread hands, wheeling and turning, circling with measured steps; and all the time the huge hollow idols, beaten with heavy clubs "to make the spirits speak," thundered death and doom. It was plainly a religious ceremony which must be fully enacted down to the last detail; but Tempest thought, as clearly as he could think in such a place and at such a time, that it could not last much longer.

"A fellow ought to say his prayers," he thought; but the thunder of the drums and the wild, shrieking song of the dancers bewildered him, and his swollen wrists and ankles hurt him so much as almost to confuse his mind.... What could he say? Only one prayer remained clear in the turmoil of his brain—just the old, old prayer that he had prayed at his mother's knee. Well, it would serve—and up above he hoped they'd understand how sorry he was ... for lots of things....

"Our Father Who art in Heaven, hallowed be Thy name. Thy kingdom come...."

It was coming, indeed! The dance had stopped.

"Thy will be done...."

What came next? He could not remember—and the savages were advancing across the square.

"Forgive us our trespasses ... and lead us not into temptation, but deliver us from evil...."

It was *now*! The women were hiding themselves in the houses, and two of the men, armed with clubs, were stepping forward.

He was only conscious of one feeling—joy that he had the courage to look the cannibals in the face as they advanced, and meet his fate "game." He hardly knew that he was still praying—

"... For Thine is the kingdom, the power, and the glory...."

Death!

It came with a blaze of light—a sound as of a wild, deep shout and the rushing of many waters—then——

Was this the end? Was it indeed death? He had felt nothing—but a man does not feel the blow that kills—and his eyes were so dazzled with a strange, blue glory that he could not see.... The rushing sound continued; it was like the thunder of hundreds of flying feet.... The light burst forth again, and yet again, and then died away, and there was a great silence. Tempest saw the hideous faces of the idols standing out in the empty square, and began to understand. He was not dead—but something had happened. What was it? He tried to break loose and sit up so as to see all round.

"Stop um little bit," said a voice, and some one drew a sharp knife across the lashings that bound his limbs, and lifted him into a sitting position.

The blinding light had almost died away now, and he could see the whole square. There was no one in it. The cannibals were gone, and the beautiful half-caste girl who had brought about his downfall—innocently, as Tempest of course supposed—was squatting beside him and putting a flask to his lips.

"Drink a little bit whisky," she said. "Good whisky; he make strong. No good stop here, you Belitani sailor-man; more better we go away too much quick."

The spirit cleared Tempest's head and put some life into his limbs. Vaiti poked him unceremoniously in the ribs as soon as she saw that he was reviving.

"Show um leg there, lively!" she ordered, dragging him by the arms. Rather to his surprise, Tempest found that he could walk, once on his feet. He wasted no time in getting away, after Vaiti's brief explanation of the blue-light stratagem, and the probable return of his enemies before very long. At something as near a run as his cramped limbs would allow, he followed her down the pathway that led away from the village—narrow, wet, and dark as a wolf's gullet—and into the comparative security of the bush, towards the advancing relief column from the *Alligator*.

It would have been no more than fitting if Vaiti, like a true heroine of romance, had vanished silently into the forest when they encountered the man-of-war's men, leaving Tempest to "turn to thank his preserver," and "find that she had disappeared." But Vaiti, as it happened, was born under the Southern Cross, where the poetry of the footlights does not flourish. So she gave the men her company on the way down as a matter of course, asked the officer in command for a cigar, smoked it and accepted half a dozen more out of his case, and made herself wonderfully pleasant—for Vaiti. She had further driven Tempest to distraction by starting a flirtation with a handsome petty officer, eaten up two emergency rations, "borrowed" some one's gold tie-pin, and very soundly boxed the ears of a leading seaman who tried to kiss her in the dark, before the long roll of the surf on the barrier reef, and the welcome glimmer of the *Alligator's* riding lights, told the tired-out party that they were safe back again. Then, like the mysterious heroine, at last she disappeared, and slipped off to the *Sybil* in a native canoe, for the reason that she did not want to be seen on board the man-of-war in a very untidy and dirty dress, without any flowers in her hair, or fresh scent on her laces. Tempest had found time to "thank his preserver" on the way down, haltingly enough; but the preserver, instead of accepting his thanks after the fashion he would have preferred, had laughed wildly and somewhat wickedly, and gone on walking right in the middle of the column, without a glance to spare for him.... Still—he thought he knew women—and.... Time would show.

\*    \*    \*    \*    \*

The rest of the wardroom did not envy Mr. Tempest his interview with the commander. It took place immediately after his return to the ship, and he came out from it with a countenance of entire inexpressiveness and extreme whiteness. One sentence—the last—was unavoidably heard by the lieutenant who followed immediately after Tempest, to deliver his report.

"Finally, Mr. Tempest—this Miss—a—Saxon—has risked her life to save your life and reputation. I think there is only one way in which you can repay her—by never seeing her again."

Tempest's answer was inaudible. But—he never did.

# CHAPTER XVII

## INVADERS IN TANNA

"What a beautiful girl! Is she one of the heathens, I wonder?" said Lady Victoria Jenkins, leaning on the rail of her yacht.

The *Alcyone* floated on a sea of living silver. The coral reefs forty feet before her keel showed like a pavement of pale turquoise in the searching splendour of the tropic moon. Close at hand loomed the dark woods and cliffs of Tanna, and above them, blotting out half the crystal broidery of the stars, rose the cone of the great volcano, crowned by a canopy of fire. So, in the days of Bougainville and of Cook, stood this southward sentinel of the wild New Hebrides, a pillar of cloud by day and a pillar of fire by night. So it stands yet, its deathless fires unquenched, its awful voice breaking the forest silences hour by hour—as the dead and gone discoverers of these distant lands saw and heard it long ago, and as those who follow us will find it in the days to come, when we and our thoughts and hopes, and adventures and loves are but a whisper in the homeless winds and a handful of dust blowing about on long-forgotten graves.

There are few volcanoes in the southern hemisphere more famous, and none less frequently visited, than the fiery cone of Tanna. The island lies thousands of miles away from everywhere, and the inhabitants are known to be almost all heathen, cannibal, and hostile to whites, although the expression of their hostility has been kept considerably in check of late years. But Lady Victoria Jenkins, daughter of the late Earl of Wessex, and wife of Mr. Abel Jenkins ("Jenkins's Perfect Pills"), is well known as a romanticist and a lover of all things unusual and strange. Mr. Abel Jenkins's income is only exceeded by that of two other commoners in England, and Mr. Abel Jenkins's ugliness and ill-temper are not exceeded by the ugliness and ill-temper of any one known to polite society. If the reader will piece these detached facts together, and consider them, he will readily understand why Lady Victoria was enjoying a tour round the world in her celebrated steam-yacht, the *Alcyone*, why she had come to look at Tanna, and why, including a good deal of miscellaneous company, the travelling party somehow was not miscellaneous enough to include Lady Victoria's husband.

The yacht had come in that afternoon after a somewhat stormy voyage from Sydney ("They call it the Pacific Ocean," said Lady Victoria plaintively, "instead of which, I have not really enjoyed a meal since we cleared the Heads"), and had instantly, by the mere fact of her dropping anchor in Sulphur Bay, denuded the whole seaboard of its population. This was because the conscience of Tanna is never quite clear, and the Tannese, struck by the conviction of sin, thought the *Alcyone* was a man-of-war. Only two kinds of ships were known to the islands, outside trading schooners: British and French warships, and the lazy little monthly steamers from Sydney, which strolled round the group once a month, picking up copra, and conveying missionaries and traders about. The *Alcyone* was not a schooner; she was certainly not the well-known "B.P." steamer; therefore she must be some new variety of man-of-war. As it happened, there was a little matter of a murdered trader on the conscience of Tanna just at that time—he had been very annoying, but a British man-of-war is prejudiced about these affairs. So the Tannese of the coast, like the modest violet of the poem, concealed their drooping heads in the shady vales of the interior, and coyly hid from view. Like the modest violet, too—only with a difference—you might, if you wished, have located them by their—— But no; this is a polite history, and the Tannese are a very impolite people. Let us change carriages.

Vaiti and her father, who had come up from Queensland with an empty ship and a full money-bag, and were just starting a fresh recruiting trip, regarded the appearance of the yacht with hearty disgust. What were the good old islands coming to if this sort of thing was to be permitted? Not a bushman would come near the beach as long as the *Alcyone* stayed, and the sprinkling of mission natives who were not afraid of the yacht were worse than useless, for they neither recruited nor encouraged their heathen friends to do so. Besides, the airs and graces of the *Alcyone* were sickening. Late dinner with low dresses and jewels; piano tinkling all the evening; clothes that looked as if they had been run hot on to the wearers, as icing is run on to a cake; sparkling glass and brasswork all over the ship, and dainty brass signal cannons, pretty as toys, and a little funnel all cream-colour and blue, and great sails white as trade-wind clouds, and a hull that sat the water like a beautiful sea-bird settled down to rest—all these unnecessary and disgusting affectations made a smart schooner like the *Sybil* look no better than a mud-scow in a marsh, for all that she was the beauty of the South Seas and the most famous ocean adventuress from 'Frisco to Hobart Town. Besides, Saxon would not stir out of his cabin while the yacht was there, having developed the lumbago that always attacked him whenever English society folk loomed on the horizon—Vaiti knew that lumbago!—and he might really have been of use about Sulphur Bay, where, for a wonder, no one had any old scores against him.

It was all most abominable, thought the "Kapitani," and she cast an unfriendly glance on the luxurious *Alcyone*, as her boat shot past the yacht in the moonlight, returning from a fruitless hunt along the coast for any stray bushman who might have heard the recruiting signal—a stick or two of dynamite set afloat on a board and exploded—and come down to the coast.

Lady Victoria's comment on the "beautiful girl" did not soften her in the least, coupled as it was with the unspeakable assumption that she was "a heathen." Probably she was, in one sense, having long ago given up all but the merest rags of religion, but it was not the accusation of moral deficiencies that galled her: it was the idea that she, Vaiti, daughter of a great Polynesian princess and a white sea-captain, should have been "evened" to the black, monkey-like, naked hags of Tanna. The resentful spirit of the half-caste burned hot within her as she steered the boat through the moonlit water. She could see Lady Victoria and her friends, a brilliant flower-show of coloured dresses and sparkling gems, leaning over the rail, and watching her as impersonally as if she were a porpoise or a shark. She could catch their comments, loudly and carelessly spoken.

"I suppose she is one of them. But she looks quite nice. See her pretty dress. She is quite decently clothed, isn't she?"

"I wonder is she a cannibal? She does not look dangerous. I would like to ask her on board, and give her some tea and cake, and things of that kind, and talk to her. Just to try and reform her from their own horrible food, you know," said Lady Victoria angelically.

"That would be so dear of you," chimed in her special sycophant and foil, a plain and elderly young woman who knew when her bread was buttered on both sides, and why.

But here the rowers—urged by a signal from Vaiti who thought she had heard about as much as she could stand without exploding—gave way vigorously, and pulled the boat out of earshot.

That was not a happy evening for any one on board the *Sybil*. Vaiti would not give out any grog for supper though it was a settled custom on the ship; would not have singing in the cabin, gloomed like a hurricane sky over the mate and boatswain's sociable game of cards until Gray, out of pure nervousness, dropped a greasy ace upon his knee, and was thereupon accused by Harris of cheating, and coarsely threatened by him with an operation usually confined to sufferers from appendicitis. At this Vaiti rose and walked out of the cabin with the air of a convent-bred princess who had never so much as heard a jibbing donkey "confounded"; and went to sit on deck near the wheel, where she stayed so long, smoking so many thin black cigars, that every one but the night watchman turned in and left her, and only the dead, dark hour of two o'clock, when the spongy heat of the island night stiffens for a while into fever-bringing chill, shook her out of her sulks and into her cabin.

When Vaiti sulked it was usually observed that things happened before very long. But on this occasion the exception seemed to rule. The disgusting yacht stayed all the next day, and the *Sybil* lay quietly at anchor on the other side of the bay. Some of the yacht people went ashore in the afternoon, and roamed timorously about the beach, wondering at the hot springs and tasting everything in the way of fruit they happened to see. (It was nearly all inedible, but none of it, by a fortunate chance, happened to be poisonous.) Lady Victoria was disappointed with her day on the whole. The natives from the mission, who had officiously attended them all day long, were unromantically clothed, clean, and English-speaking. The wild savages did not appear; and there were one or two other mishaps of an entirely unromantic kind.

"How did you enjoy it, darling?" asked the plain young woman of Lady Victoria, when the daring pioneers returned.

Mr. Jenkins's partner shook out her soiled tussore silk disgustedly.

"It was untidy and ugly and nasty," she declared; "and when I sat down under a great pineapple tree all covered with fruit, and said that I was realising one of my dreams, Jack de Coverley laughed at me, and said it was only a pandamn-us, or something else profane, and that pineapples grew on the ground. And when we started to walk among the palms, and I was saying that I had always dreamed of wandering softly by a coral strand and seeing the cocoanuts drop into my hands, something as big as a horse's head suddenly thundered down like a bombshell from a hundred feet high, and buried itself in the sand at my feet with such a fearful shock that I jumped a yard away and screamed like anything! So then the missionary came out, and said he wondered I wasn't killed; and if you'll believe me, it was nothing but a horrible nut! And the coral strand was pretty enough, all over little bits of branching coral stuff; but why doesn't anyone ever tell you that coral strands burn all the skin off your nose and blacken you into a nigger? We're going up the volcano to-morrow—the missionary says it's quite safe—and I'm sure I hope it's true, but one never knows. Darling, if I die, see that the new Lafayette photo is sent to the papers—not on any account the other; and I like Latin crosses on graves, I think; Carrara marble, very thick, and just one short text, something nice, like 'They were lovely and pleasant in their lives'—you know."

... "'And in death they were not divided,'" finished the plain young woman with mechanical piety.... "Darling! dearest! what have I said? What is the matter?"

"Now you *have* done it!" roared Mr. de Coverley, who was rather a well-bred, but sometimes rather a vulgar young man. "Not divided! Oh, great Scott! Oh, my eye! Oh, I'll die of laughing! Hold me up! Never mind, Vic; I'll see you aren't divided, or cooked either—trust to me!"

*   *   *   *   *

Vaiti was still in a speechless state of sulks when she started off the next morning into the interior, to recruit on her own account. It was not a very safe thing to do, but the bushmen would not come down to the coast, and the *Sybil* could not hang out indefinitely, since the doubtful character of her methods had given the French and English Commissioners of the islands a nasty habit of asking questions about her. Saxon, who had relinquished his lumbago to go off into the hills at a safe distance from the yacht, wanted to make his daughter accompany him; but Vaiti simply laughed at him, and departed with a guide seduced from the mission towards a village lying a mile or two above the volcano. She preferred the glory of working on her own account, and besides, it doubled the chances of recruits.

She knew the Tannese nature well, so she dressed herself for her part in a robe of scarlet sateen, with liberal necklaces of different coloured trade beads, and stuck a couple of tomahawks in her sash, besides an ornamented sheath-knife. Across her splendid young bosom she slung an incongruous-looking bandolier of cartridges, designed apparently for the slaughter of elephants; and a smart magazine rifle, carried over her shoulder, completed the outfit. All these valuables, though designed to assist her plans by suggesting the enormous store of desirable goods possessed by the recruiters, were almost as likely to assist her to a sudden and unprovided end, by reason of the natives' covetousness. She took her chance of this, however; Vaiti was used to taking chances. It is easier than most people suppose to take the risk of being killed every day of your life. In the strange places of the earth, where such things are a common happening, men do not look upon the inevitable end after the pursy, secretive, never-mention-it fashion of Peckham and Brixton. Death is just death in the earth's wild places—yours to-day, mine to-morrow—a thing to walk with shoulder to shoulder, to meet face to face at noonday; in any case, to make no bones of it until it makes bones of you; and after that circumstances will keep you from complaining if you feel like it.

It was a long, hot walk up to the village. A "walk" is mostly a scramble about the uncleared New Hebrides, where roads are mere foot-wide cracks and canyons in the dense forest growth, and level ground apparently does not exist. Besides, a bandolier of cartridges and an assortment of small arms are rather heavy jewellery for such a climate. Vaiti, however, possessed the enviable gift of never looking, or apparently feeling, hot or tired; and she swung along at an unvarying pace that caused the unlawfully enticed mission native, who had waxed fat and lazy, to regret his enticement and wish himself back in the mission school writing copies, instead of slaving up and down precipitous gullies in the rear of a woman-devil who did not know what it was to want a rest.

At long last, however, the reedwork fence of the village came in sight, and they entered the open square, shaded by an immense banyan tree and surrounded by low, ugly huts, all roof and no wall, like all the mountain villages of Tanna. There were sentries perched up in the trees outside the gate, and others squatted on the ground at every entrance, their rifles ready in the crook of the elbow. Within, the dusty tan-coloured square, quivering under the pitiless fire of the white-hot sky, was all alive with moving figures—ugly women in brief grass skirts humped out into swaying bustles; young boys with murderous little faces, and full-sized rifles; wild-looking men, with thick hair twined into myriads of tiny strings ending in a great bush on the shoulders, stripes of scarlet paint on their faces, and no clothing save their native impudence and a cartridge belt—all seething about in a very bee-hive of excitement and alarm. As for the rifle-barrels, they were bobbing about like piano-jumpers all over the square, and every weapon was cocked and loaded.

Vaiti saw at a glance that they were expecting an attack, and picking out a native who could speak English, asked what the trouble was. The man replied that they feared the little man-of-war down below, but that they were entirely innocent. Questioned further, they said naïvely that they had never eaten a white man, and that none of them were low cannibals in any case. Vaiti, who had not heard of this little affair before, saw her chance.

"No good you speak alonga that fellow way," she said, using the *bêche-de-mer* talk that some of the Tannese understood; for Vaiti, like many half-castes, could handle almost any dialect or corruption of a dialect, though she could not speak decent English or French. "I savvy plenty, you eatum one fellow white man. By'n by, big fellow man-of-war come, shoot you all-a-same one pig, all-a-same one blind box [flying fox], burn altogether house belong you. Very good you come alonga Saxon ship, go Queensland; then you all right."

"No eatum," persisted the man (who was the professional talking-man or orator of the village), with a coy smile.

Vaiti's nose was keen, and she had already guessed something by its aid. She marched straight across the square into a little yam-house, and pointed to a small parcel done up in green banana-leaf and tied with cocoanut sinnet. Five toes and an instep protruded from one end. The game had been well hung, as the Tannaman likes it to be, and there was no mistaking the fact of its presence in any sense.

The talking-man giggled like a school-girl caught consuming surreptitious chocolates.

"Eatum jus' little-fellow bit," he allowed, with a bad-child chuckle. The other men took up the laugh, and the village resounded with a roar like the bellowing of a herd of bulls.

Vaiti, seeing her advantage, stepped out into the square and began to talk, marching to and fro in Tannese fashion as she spoke. The sun cast dancing spangles on her many-coloured beads as she moved, and threw back darts of fire from her heavy bandolier. One arm emphasised her remarks with sweeping gesture; in the other the tall rifle pounded the earth with its stock, marking the points of her discourse. The fat, stolid mission native watched her with staring eyes and open mouth, and the chiefs gloomed at her under sullen savage brows, evidently impressed, but restive.

The sum of her discourse was that they and their women would do well to come down with her to the schooner, recruit at once, and fly to a land of safety where men-of-war never came, where Tanna people reclined all day under the shade of banyan and banana, picked a little cane for their employers occasionally, lived upon tinned meat and sugared tea, and eventually returned loaded with riches in the shape of rifles, cartridges, cotton, and knives. There was a good deal more of the same highly-coloured stuff. This was old business to the people of the *Sybil.*

The talking-man, also strutting backwards and forwards, Tanna fashion, in a kind of continual country dance with the glittering vision from the ship, answered now and then. It was very well to talk about recruiting, and perhaps some of them might go if they got lots of tinned salmon and "bisketti" to eat before they went on board, and promise of rifles to be paid the tribe when the bargain was complete. But they did not believe that the new ship was not a little man-of war, and until she was gone they would not go down to the coast—no, not even to bathe, although they had all decided to have a bath soon, for the weather was hot and their skins were like the bark of trees, and it was now about ten moons since they had had their last bath.

At this Vaiti's eyes lit up, for she suddenly saw a plan, a plan which might give her a score of recruits, drive the objectionable yacht out of Sulphur Bay, and pay off every rankling insult inflicted by the *Alcyone* and her people. But the savages were watching her, so she veiled her eyes with her long lashes, and replied carelessly:

"All that very good. To-morrow, small-fellow man-of-war he go 'way; then you coming longa schooner. To-day, what name [why?] you no go wash big water 'long place one-fellow-fire stop? Very good place that. Suppose you going, I come up from schooner, bring plenty-plenty tucker. Plenty-plenty bulimacow [beef], bisketti, tucker belong white man, cost ten rifle. All the Tannaman he eat; by'n-by he stop lie down, he break, so much he eat."

This tempting picture had its effect, backed up by a few presents of beads and cartridges. The Tannamen agreed that the plain below the burning mountain, where a wide, stagnant lake spread out its dull expanse, would do for a bathing place, short of the impossible shore, and they chuckled with joyous anticipation of the feast. They also agreed, rather doubtfully, to embark as soon as the "man-of-war" was gone; and it seemed evident that a fair number would at least come down and negotiate on board the schooner after which—well, the *Sybil's* smart heels would do the rest.

# CHAPTER XVIII

## A CANNIBAL PARTY

Vaiti went off to get ready the feast, telling the natives that they might follow her before long, as everything would be ready soon; and they might trust her, the great Kapitani, that it would be a feast such as no Tannaman, not even of those who had served in Queensland, had ever witnessed in his wildest dreams.

The mission native being a rather weak-kneed convert, and anxious to enjoy a good heathen gossip with his old companions, wanted very much to stay on in the village. But that was just what Vaiti did not want, so she drove him out in front of her like a fat and nervous sheep, hastening his movements all the way down with occasional reminders from the butt of her rifle. He had given her certain information about a picnic at the foot of the volcano, arranged by the people of the yacht for that afternoon, and she did not want him to share his news with the men of the village and cause them, perhaps, to put two and two together where he himself had failed to do so. She despatched him therefore to his own town on the coast, and saw that he went, before herself turning off in the direction of the track that led to the volcano.

Near to the lake there lies a curious little valley with a soft, clean flooring of black volcanic sand and sheltering walls of green pandanus. Here, shaded from the burning heat, yet close to the volcano plain, was the only possible place for the picnickers to enjoy their meal. Beyond lay only a lurid plateau of red and yellow lava beds, curdled and coiled as they had flowed down from the crater lip long ago; a desert of black ash and sand, and a dark, wicked, smoking, rumbling cone in the centre of all. Not a native would have climbed the cone for all the goods in the *Sybil's* hold; it was the mouth of hell, they said, and full of devils of every kind. But they were not afraid of the valley below, within safe limits, and even if they had been, the feast and the bathe after it were attractive enough to conquer a little nervousness.

As Vaiti had anticipated, there were several picnic baskets stowed under a tree in the valley, and a big wine hamper as well. Four mission natives, who had acted as guides and carried up the provisions, were lying on their stomachs in the shade, smoking and talking.

It was essential to get them out of the way, and time was short. Vaiti did not waste any unnecessary words. She simply pointed her rifle at the men and told them to clear. They cleared, howling, and she was left alone.

With quick, neat hands she unpacked the hampers, spread the cloth, and laid out the food. It was a goodly display—hams and tongues and fowls, cold meats, pies, cakes, tarts, fruits, and tinned dainties of every kind. There was plenty of champagne, also a supply of whisky and soda. She set all the bottles in a row, and looked with satisfaction upon the glittering array. Then she went up to the edge of the plain and looked at the crater. No one was yet in sight. The exploring party at that moment were on the other side of the cone, standing on the black lip of an appalling gulf eight hundred feet deep and half a mile across; looking down, awe-struck and amazed, upon colossal fire fountains that uplifted their gory spray three hundred feet in the air, and listening to the heart-shaking thunders of the volcano's awful voice, as from time to time that terrifying note of illimitable force and fury made the whole plain tremble and echoed far out to sea.... It was indeed no wonder that the ignorant Tannamen feared to ascend the cone.

Vaiti sat down at the edge of the plain, and watched till she saw a number of many-coloured dots creeping down the black pyramid in its centre. Then she suddenly lay down upon the ashy ground, and writhed with silent laughter. People were in the habit of saying that Vaiti had no more sense of humour than the jibboom of her father's ship. They might have modified that judgment, could they have seen her now.

*    *    *    *    *

Lady Victoria Jenkins had enjoyed her morning very much indeed. She had dressed for the ascent in a mountaineering costume that combined equal suggestions of "Carmen" and the Alpine Club, and gave great opportunities to her ankles. She had been helped up the cone by four devoted admirers, all at once, and had come down it at a wild running slide, ably braked by two strong hands of two or three others who wanted to have their turn. The other women had trodden on their skirts, and torn them, burned and cut their foolish boots, and also got unbecomingly hot and out of breath, because there was not nearly one man apiece to help them up, after Lady Victoria had annexed all the best. It must be allowed that the men were the weak point of the *Alcyone's* travelling party. Mr. de Coverley and his set were "dear boys" and charming companions, no doubt, but they were not quite as manly as some of the ladies. Lady Vic and her companions did not attract the best sort of men, as a rule.

They were all very hungry when they reached the plain, and thirsty with a thirst unknown outside the tropics. All the way across the baking black sand and the tinkling lava beds, "one fair vision ever fled" before the eyes of the party—vision of gold-necked champagne bottles lying coolly embedded in icebaskets; of topaz-coloured jellies, trembling on silver dishes; of flaky, savoury pies, and delicate cold meats, and crisp green salads concocted as only the hand of the *Alcyone's chef* could concoct them.

It seemed as if that plain would never end, but it did end at last, and a green fringe of pandanus announced the beginning of the bush. The elderly young lady and most of the others were making excellent time ahead, and they reached the verge of the plain some little while before Lady Victoria and Mr. de Coverley came to it. The latter pair, as it happened, were really not thinking very much about their lunch, because a still more interesting matter absorbed their attention.

"Not understood!" Mr. de Coverley was saying bitterly. "And so we die and go down to the grave—not understood! The pathos of it!"

"We are never understood," sighed Lady Victoria, patting the side waves of her "transformation" to see that it was on straight. "We women, especially. And those who should understand us best of all are so often——"

"Exactly—so they are. But, Lady Victoria—Victoria!—there are some who are different; there are men, rare souls, who——"

"What in Heaven's name is the matter?" interrupted the misunderstood one, stopping dead in her tracks (literally, for the sand was deep) and staring at the edge of the bush.

From the valley below the plain had just risen a long, loud shriek, followed by another and another, and then by a burst of laughter that sounded scarcely human. The other members of the party had disappeared, but it was clear that something had happened.

"Good God, the savages!" exclaimed Lady Victoria; and she began to run. Let it be stated, for the credit of her race and name, that she ran towards the sound. As for Mr. de Coverley....

But this story is not about Mr. de Coverley. If it were, it would be interesting to tell why the Sydney steamer that called at Sulphur Bay two days later found an unexpected passenger waiting at the trader's, and why Lady Victoria and Mr. Abel Jenkins, of Jenkins's Perfect Pills, became eventually reconciled and lived the life of a model couple. As things are, it must be enough to state that Mr. Jack de Coverley turned and ran away at the sound of the shouts—ran right across the plain into the bush at the other side—ran as far as he could get, and did not come back at all—and thereby ran once and for ever out of the life of the lady whom he "understood."

Lady Victoria, speeding in the opposite direction, reached the edge of the little valley in a very few minutes, and, looking over, beheld what was certainly the strangest sight she had encountered in all her varied life.

Round about the elaborately-laid luncheon were squatting a dozen or so of naked brown savages, painted, feathered, and slashed with ornamental scars. A few women, clad only in a six-inch fringe of grass, stood behind them, eyeing the eatables eagerly, but not daring to touch them while their masters fed. The talking-man, a big, hulking savage with a huge bush of hair, and a match-box stuck in each ear-lobe, had buried his face in the savoury interior of a boned turkey, and was gnawing out the stuffing. The principal chief, one hand in a dish of Spanish cream and the other in a chicken curry, was casting double supplies into his mouth with the regularity of a patent feed-machine. A fat young fighting man, with nose and forehead painted scarlet, and white ashes in his hair, had tucked a ham under one arm, and was sitting on a peach pie, with intent to secure as many good things as possible, while he hastily worried large mouthfuls off the forequarter of lamb he was holding in both hands. Another man was drinking mint sauce out of the silver sauceboat with horrible grimaces; his neighbour, having captured a handful of maraschino jelly, fast melting in the sun, was industriously rubbing it on his hair; and a grizzly old fellow, with a monkey-like face, was half-choking himself over a soufflé, which he was trying to swallow case and all. The necks of the champagne bottles were all knocked off, and from engraved wine-cases, empty entrée-dishes, and dredged-out tins the savages were drinking Lady Victoria's excellent wines with every appearance of satisfaction. Between mouthfuls they stopped to look at the party from the yacht, and to roar with laughter at their evident fright. Too terrified even to run away, the voyagers, in their dainty frocks and smart white suits, stood huddling together for protection, the women crying, the men looking rather white and foolish, for every Tannaman had a loaded rifle slung to his side, and there was not so much as a saloon pistol among the whites. A few yards off Vaiti stood, regarding the whole scene with an expressionless countenance that covered a good deal of quiet enjoyment. She knew, if the visitors did not, that the cannibal bushmen were really not at all a bad lot of fellows when you knew them, and that the yacht party, against whom they had no grudge, were perfectly safe. In fact, the Tannamen merely thought these oddly-behaved whites were a new party of missionaries, and were quite ready to be civil to them, since they thought all the mission people harmless, if eccentric.

But the true inwardness of the situation not being apparent, the *Alcyone's* guests were very frightened indeed.

"P-perhaps if we go away very quietly, they won't f-follow us," said a wealthy young stockbroker, who had retained a little presence of mind, though his teeth were chattering in his head.

"Oh, let us! Victoria, save me! Oh, what shall we do?" wailed the elderly young lady, rushing up the bank and flinging her arms round the mistress of the violated feast. Lady Victoria, though white as her own Belfast linen collar, kept her head fairly well. She saw that Vaiti was not one of the invaders, and called to her. "Do you speak English? What are we to do? Will they kill us?" she asked.

Vaiti walked over to her with the bearing of a stage duchess, and favoured her with a fashionable high handshake that was the one thing wanting to complete the insanity of the whole impossible scene. A new idea had suddenly struck her—a fresh spark of mischief was lit. With an immovable countenance she replied:

"No kill you, I think. Suppose you want go 'way all right by'n-by, very good I think you sit down, eatum dinner alonga those fellow—then they think you all right, let you go home, no kill."

"Oh, Victoria, anything to please them!" sobbed the elderly young lady.

"Yes—a—I think we'd better do anything we can to get into their good graces, since we're not armed," submitted the stockbroker.

Vaiti exchanged a few words with the Tannese. She explained that these white people had come a long way, and were very hungry. The Melanesian has not many virtues, but hospitality is certainly one of them; and a man who may be planning to dine off you himself to-morrow will certainly not refuse you half of his own leaf of yams to-day. The Tannese were delighted at the chance of sharing their good fortune with the white chiefs, even in spite of the latter's extremely silly manners, and they beckoned to them at once to come and sit down.

Thereafter took place a scene incapable of description by mortal pen. The chief took his head out of the turkey, chewed off a leg, and grinningly handed it to Lady Victoria. The young warrior got off the pie, disembowelled it with one scoop of the hand that had not known water "for ten moons," and laid its interior in the elderly young lady's lap. Another knowingly poured out a champagne glass of Worcester sauce and handed it to the stockbroker, while the much-bitten lump of mutton that was at that moment circling from mouth to mouth, native-fashion, was hospitably passed on to all the whites. Driven by fear, they tried to swallow something; choked in the effort, made futile remarks to each other, laughed nervous laughs, and all the time watched with eyes of utmost apprehension the dusky hosts who were thus entertaining them with their own audaciously ravished goods. And above the crazy party the burning Tanna sun beat down, and the great volcano-cone far across the plain smoked and thundered.

It had been Vaiti's design to dismiss them in peace by and by, assured that their compliance had saved their lives, and anxious to make steam out of Sulphur Bay as soon as was reasonably possible. Fate, however, reserved a more dramatic ending to the entertainment, And it was "all along of" that talking-man.

The cannibal native is invariably shy of displaying his tastes before whites, since people who do not share the "point of view" are so frequently prejudiced. Therefore the talking-man did not open a certain small green parcel tied up with sinnet string, which he had brought down with him from the mountain village. A feast in the hand is worth two in the pandanus-bush, thought the talking-man, so he brought his *bonne bouche* with him for dessert and said nothing about it. And thereby came the end.

For Lady Victoria, unable to swallow the clawed and chewed morsels pressed upon her by dirt-encrusted hands, began to hunt despairingly about for something that she could really eat, so that she should not offend the dangerous monsters who surrounded her.

"Isn't there anything clean to be had?" she asked the stockbroker anxiously. "I can't eat—and yet we must! What are we to do?"

The stockbroker, who had once been to Honolulu, and thought he knew something about native foods, spied the packet of green banana-leaf, and reached out for it.

"This'll be some of their own boiled yam," he said. "Natives always do it up like this. You can eat it all right if you scrape it with a knife. Allow me."

Before the talking-man could stretch out his filthy claw to stop him, the Englishman had cut the sinnet string, the parcel had burst open, and right into the middle of a half-demolished chicken pie fell a large white foot, cut off at the ankle, nicely browned across the instep and all crackled on the toes.

There was a wild shriek from the women, a splutter of horrified exclamations from the men, a boiling up of white petticoats like to the breaking of a wave on a pebbly shore, and then nothing but a diminishing string of rapidly trotting figures, each woman hand in hand with a man who was dragging her along far away, farther and farther, down the long, black, sandy path into the bush. Then ... they were gone.

Vaiti stood on the bank to look after them, and laughed quietly.

"Now I think we keep Sulphur Bay all our own self," she said.

As for the Tannamen, they rolled on the ground with laughter, and then picked the dainty morsel out of the chicken pie and ate it up.

# CHAPTER XIX

## THE RIVAL PRINCESSES

It was full mid-day when the schooner *Sybil* dropped anchor off Liali Island. The hot season was at its height. The long, white coral strand blazed in the sun, the moated lagoon was raw emerald, the waveless outer sea blue fire. Beyond the beach stretched a green, grassy lawn, dotted with quaintly-shaped Norfolk pines, tall palms, and feather-tressed ironwood trees; and against its enamelled background rose a palace like a picture in a fairy-tale—white, long-windowed, lofty-towered, and crowned with a crimson flag set below a gilded vane.

Vaiti, standing on the break of the poop, with the inevitable cigar between her fingers, looked critically at the island, and liked it well. A mere little matter of kidnapping somebody's indentured labourers—the sort of thing that any gentleman with an extensive island practice might easily find himself obliged to do—had brought about her father's expulsion from the New Hebrides labour trade, and obliged him to seek new fields for the activities of the notorious and naughty *Sybil*. Saxon himself was virtuously indignant, Vaiti not particularly sorry. She was getting tired of the gloomy feverish New Hebrides and their ugly savages. The Eastern Pacific was her heart's home after all, semi-Polynesian as she was; and even the wild excitement of the cruel western isles could not hold her away very long. So when Saxon was wavering between the advantages of strictly illegal gun-running in the Solomons and honest trading about the Liali group (which had just wrecked its native schooner, and was open to employ a successor), Vaiti's influence went for once on the side of peace and virtue, and the course was set for Liali. The group was new to both father and daughter, but was none the less attractive on that account, since all over the wide island world the *Sybil* and her owners were best loved and most warmly welcomed where they were least known.

The Liali group, as many people in the Southern hemisphere agree, offers the nearest possible approach to comic opera known off the actual stage. Liali itself, the chief island, is as pretty as a toy-box, and quite extraordinarily theatrical in appearance. Its handsome, merry, brown people wear the most picturesque costume in the Pacific—a knee-length kilt of fine cashmere, girded by a deep sash of pure silk, and worn with a silken or cashmere shirt or a graceful sleeveless tunic, according to sex—all in the most vivid of sea- and flower-colour. Liali is civilised after a fashion. It goes barefoot and barelegged, sits on mats, lives in reed-woven houses devoid of furniture, worships a sacred lizard on the sly, and sometimes breaks out openly into club-fights and devil-dances. But it has a king, and a palace and a Parliament, a brass band, and quite a number of very active Nonconformist churches, run by white missionaries, who find that "labouring" among the well-off and amiable Lialians is a task in which the meritorious martyrdom of missionary life can be combined with quite a number of pleasant alleviations.

Nothing in Liali is entirely what it seems. The palace, when one comes close to it, is perceived to be built of painted wood, like a "practicable" scene in a theatre. The Parliament never passes any laws, because the Lords, who are chiefs, always on principle throw out every bill introduced by the vulgar Commons, just to "teach" them. The Prime Minister is oftener in prison for *lèse majestè* than out of it, and several Chancellors of the Exchequer have been transported to the Colonies for theft. But there is a real throne in the palace, all crimson velvet and gilt wood, and a wonderful gold crown (the verdigris is cleaned off it with a wad of cocoanut husks by the Chief Equerry every Saturday afternoon), and when the King goes out in state he wears a purple velvet train, held up by two pages in tights and plumes, and a marvellous ermined robe, all exactly like the Savoy Theatre in the consulship of Gilbert and Sullivan. On occasions not of state he sits cross-legged upon the palace parquet, clad in a shirt and a kilt, and plays *écarté* with his native guards.

There are a few colonial traders in Liali, and a dozen or so of the English "legion that never was listed"—just such as one finds in all the odd corners of the Pacific—talkative, plausible, thin and nervous, given to avoid home topics and discourse with awful fluency upon small local politics; hospitable, restless and lazy, and usually married more or less to some dark beauty of the islands, who has grown as fat as a feather bed and spends a fortune on store muslins.

These, as a matter of course, took possession of the *Sybil's* people at once, hardly waiting for the schooner to cast anchor before they were alongside with their boats. Saxon and Vaiti were swept ashore immediately, and begged to make their home in half-a-dozen different houses. With a fine sense of the fitting, Saxon selected Bob Peter's public-house, misnamed hotel, and immediately held a *levée* in the bar, wearing his smartest Auckland suit (not paid for, and not likely to be) and looking, with his heavy, old-fashioned cavalry moustache, blonde-grey hair, and well set-up though rather bloated figure, quite like a somewhat seedy Milor on his travels. (And, as a matter of fact.... But that was Saxon's long-buried secret, and must not be told.)

Vaiti, splendidly attired in a flowing island robe of yellow silk, with a gold chain twisted through her misty black hair, sat in the midst of a court of her own, and drank expensive pink lemonade to her soul's content. She was revelling in the sights, the sounds, the smells of the dear eastern islands once more. She had a necklace of perfumed red berries round her neck, and white "tieré" flowers behind each ear, and the well-remembered scent almost intoxicated her. Outside she could hear the boom of a dancing-chant, broken by interludes of clapping; and from the very next house, a big native reed-built structure, came now and then in the quieter moments the sonorous voice of a Lialian man calling out the names at a kava-drinking.

The double soul that is the curse of the half-caste surged within the girl.... This, this, this, and all it meant—how she loved it! And yet, the wild, fierce life of the western islands; the chance, the risk, the strong wine of danger, adventure, power! The two natures of the soldier of fortune and the sensuous island princess who had given her birth, fought together in her heart.... If one could eat one's cake and have it! If one could sleep all day, crowned with flowers, under the singing casuarina trees, and yet be the daring sea-queen, the "Kapitani" of the *Sybil*, if only....

Vaiti shook herself impatiently in her hammock chair, and asked for ginger beer with sugar in it. She hated thinking, and felt as if she were going mad when the half-white brain in her pretty dusky head took a strange fit of sober industry. Swift, instinctive plotting and planning were one thing, deliberate reflection quite another.... Ugh! she must be sick.... And for once the temperate Vaiti said yes to the inevitable offer of "a stick in it," as her ginger beer was handed to her by an eager admirer.

The "sickness" passed away, and she began to listen and watch in her old fashion, smiling all the time to the compliments and sweet sayings that were being poured into her ears. A trader was telling her father all about the latest dynastic crisis in the monarchy, and Saxon was not even pretending to listen. The affairs of "niggers" never interested him, unless there was a question of immediate profit ahead.

"You see," said the trader, "King Napoleon Timothy Te Paea III., which is his full title, wants for to get married. He's thirty, and there's no heir. And there being just the two Lialian princesses that wasn't his sisters—Mahina and Litia—what does he do but go and propose to both of them, and, of course, gets snapped up like winkin' by the two. It's no small potatoes being Queen of Liali, mind you. Te Paea gets lots of money out of the fruit, and copra taxes, and then the Crown lands is half the island, there's presents besides. And he's a real king if he is coffee-coloured—why, the kings of Liali goes back hundreds of years before Captain Cook, and he was in Henry Eighth's time, wasn't he? And if you was to see the pink satin chairs in the throne-room, and the phonographs, and musical-boxes, and albums, and lookin'-glasses, and the lovely wax flowers in cases, and real hand-painted oil pictures—ah! it's a good job, is Te Paea's, and either Mahina or Litia's going to be a very lucky girl. What he'd like, you see, is to marry both of them, same as his old grandfather—only he married nine, he did. But the King's a Methody, good as they make them—when he don't forget, or want a spree—

and of course the missionaries won't hear of his havin' two queens. And, says he, Mahina's real fat; there's nothing mean about Mahina; she fills the eye, says he, and that's what a Lialian likes, for they don't hold with any sort of stinginess, says he. But Litia, he says, has eyes like the buttons on his Auckland boots, they're so round and black and bright, says he, and she walks for all the world like a lovely young mutton-bird, says he. And what's a king to do, with both the girls' relations fighting and squabbling over him like land-crabs fighting over a bit of fish, and he himself liking them both, and the girls clean mad for him—because, you see, Te Paea he's a handsome fellow, and when he's got his military uniform on, and all his orders and medals what he drew out himself on paper, and got made in Sydney, he's a fancy man, he is. The wedding's to be in three weeks, and the invites is being printed down in Auckland all in silver, with a blank to write the bride's name in—and the House of Lords has bought the bride's dress for her, which is what the Kings says it's their right to do, according to custom,—and no one knows which he's going to marry, and no more does he. And it's my belief that there'll be war over it, before all's said and done, for Mahina's people say they'll burn down every village belonging to Litia's tribe, and Litia's folks say they'll kill Mahina's people's cattle and cut up their gardens. That's the way things are, and you may take my word it's a pretty kettle of fish."

"What are you giving for copra at present?" asked Saxon, yawning unrestrainedly. And the conversation turned at once to the inevitable trading "shop."

A few days afterwards the *Sybil* spread her wings and started for Waiwai, the outermost of the Liali islands. She was to make the whole round of the group afterwards, and might not be back for some weeks, so that it seemed likely that Saxon would miss the festivities of the King's wedding. This Vaiti declared was no reason why she should miss them, and she insisted on being left behind. Saxon was not too well pleased, for if he had a remnant of conscience left, it was connected with the care of his daughter, and he did not quite care about leaving her alone in a group to which they were both strangers. But Vaiti promised to behave like a saint, and furthermore said that she would stay with one of the married traders, and not in the native villages. She also added that she meant to stay anyhow, and that it was no use making a fuss.

So the *Sybil* sailed away out of Liali harbour, and became a little pearl-coloured pinhead on the blue horizon, and then melted quite away. And Vaiti went to the tin-roofed shanty belonging to Neumann, the fat German trader, who had married a Lialian wife, and was received with the unquestioning hospitality of the islands.

Nobody, among either whites or natives, could talk of anything but the King's matrimonial affairs. Mahina and Litia both appeared in Neumann's parlour more than once, sat on the floor, drank black tea with a handful of sugar in it, and related their several woes at length. They did not come together, except once, when Litia, walking in unexpectedly, found Mahina there, crying into her teacup, and telling Neumann's wife that the King had given Litia a beautiful chemise, all trimmed with lace, only the day before, and that in consequence she considered him a monster and a perjured villain, although she knew perfectly well that he meant nothing whatever by it. What was a chemise? He had sent her two pounds of stick tobacco the Sunday before last. She would show Litia yet that the King was her King, and nobody else's.

Litia, entering at this point, wasted no words, but simply buried her hands in Mahina's curly black masses of hair, and dragged her, shrieking, across the floor. Neumann interfered, and parted them; but Mahina flew at Litia immediately after, ripped open her dress with one clutch, and disclosed the royal gift chastely embracing Litia's lovely form. With a howl of anger, the rival seized the chemise in both hands; there was a scuffle, a scream, a rending noise, and Litia stood up in the middle of the room, a gold-bronze statue, shedding tears of rage, while Mahina, running out on to the verandah, tore the offending garment into strips and rags, and cast them upon the road. Litia, rushing out after her, stood upon the steps clad with wrath as with a garment (and with extremely little else), explaining her wrongs to an interested and sympathetic native crowd, until the Methodist missionary happened to come by, and told her that unless she went in and dressed herself at once, she might safely count upon eventually finding herself in a place where dress would be very much at a discount ... or words to that effect. So Litia went in, and Mahina went away, escorted by a strong cousinly "tail"; and afterwards Neumann, enveloped in oracular clouds of smoke, remarked sleepily that the princesses were the greatest nuisance on the island, and that he believed the King would run away from the whole set if he could, for he was "by-nearly mad-driven on account of their so-tiresome ways, and feared-himself to choose, because the one that he not married had would cause to make war by her people against the one he married should."

During the whole of the fight, Vaiti remained perfectly unmoved on a cane lounge in the corner of the room, uninterruptedly puffing rings of blue smoke at the ceiling. Not a detail had escaped her, all the same, nor did she miss a word of Neumann's remarks. And they made her think.

In the afternoon, the dull thud of galloping hoofs along the grass street made Mrs. Neumann run to the door. She called loudly to Vaiti to come.

"It is the King," she said.

A small victoria, drawn by two spirited blacks, was tearing up the street. Seated alone in it was an extraordinary and notable figure—Napoleon Timothy Te Paea III., King of Liali. He was six feet four inches in height, and over eighteen stone in weight. He wore a scarlet cloth uniform coat, blazing with gold, and his heavy, handsome brown face, with its weak, small mouth, and black eyes almost too large and soft for a man, was shaded by a white sun helmet with a wide gold band.

He drove furiously, looking neither to right nor to left, and, passing the house like a gorgeous whirlwind, was instantly lost in the casuarina forest beyond.

"That is the King, then?" said Vaiti. The Lialian language came almost as easily to her as her own, being only one of the dialects of the great Maori tongue that covers a good two-thirds of the island world.

"Yes," said Neumann's wife, "that is the King. And very little any of us have seen of him lately. He is afraid of the trouble he has got himself into; he shuts himself up all the time, and sees no one but his guards, and just sends a present now and then, first to one girl then to the other. And when he drives to take the air, he flies along like that, so that no one can stop and speak to him. He is terribly shy of strangers; I think it was because the *Sipila* was here that he did not come out at all last week."

"Is it such a very good thing for the princess he will marry?" asked Vaiti, playing with a yellow alamanda flower.

"Very, very good indeed," replied the Lialian impressively. "She will have a gold crown to wear on her head, and sit on a red velvet and gold throne beside the King, and have the most beautiful satin dresses from Sydney, and all her chemises will have lace and ribbons on them. And as soon as the King buys another schooner for himself and Liali, she will travel in it with him whenever she likes, for sometimes he will go to Samoa, to stay with King Malietoa, or he will sail a whole week to Mbau in Fiji, and then Princess Thakombau and the Prince of Kandavu make feasts and dances for him, and the Kovana [governor] gives a real 'papalangi' dinner for him, with champagne and a band. And as for what she will have to eat at home, it is past telling, for in the palace there is no count whatever made of tinned salmon and biscuit, and she may have a sackful of sugar at every meal, and a whole roast pig every day. She may eat till she falls asleep, and then wake up to eat. Ah, it is a good thing for the princess who marries the King, whichever she may be!"

"I think you will be thirsty if you talk so much," said Vaiti rather rudely. "I am thirsty myself with only listening to you. Go and make some kava for me."

Mrs. Neumann, who had been rather proud to have Vaiti staying with her—since her rank as a princess of Atiu counted for a good deal among the island races—began to dislike her visitor soon after this, and to wish her well away. Vaiti was not an angel in the house at the best of times, and she did not trouble to make herself pleasant just then. Indeed, one would almost have thought she was trying to pick a quarrel. And, as that sort of effort rarely goes unrewarded, it is not astonishing to learn that the quarrel came before long—a bitter, loud-tongued dispute that left Mrs. Neumann sobbing in a fat, frightened heap on the floor, and Vaiti, silent but stormy, packing up her camphorwood box to depart.

Neumann, being afraid of Saxon's possible anger, tried to keep her, but she laughed in his face, and went on packing. There was an empty native house—little more than a palm-leaf hut, once tenanted by a Chinese trader—standing by the road about halfway through the great casuarina forest; a lonely, ramshackle place, used and wanted by nobody. There and there only Vaiti would go, taking mats and cooking pots with her, to stay until her father came back. When some of the islanders betrayed meddlesome curiosity as to her motives, and the missionaries declared they scented scandal, Vaiti silenced and terrified the one, and convinced the others that she was hopelessly beyond the pale, by giving out that she was something of a witch, and meant to go into the forest to gather and prepare certain powerful charms. These, she said, would injure only her enemies, but were altogether powerless to hurt anyone who spoke well of her. In consequence, the evil tongues of Liali received a sudden check.

Furthermore, Vaiti, neglecting the half-castes and the whites, began with considerable art to make herself popular among the natives. She dressed herself Liali fashion, and arranged her hair after the island modes. She joined in all their interminable boating journeys and picnics, and was never tired of sitting cross-legged on the ground, waving her arms and head in time with a hundred others, and chanting Lialian songs that lasted an afternoon apiece. After dark, she was often to be seen out on the reef, with a torch and a fishing spear making an exhibition of piscatorial skill that astonished even the Lialians themselves. When there was an unmissionary dance in some big chief-house, Vaiti was always there, decked with wreaths and flower necklaces, and polished with cocoanut oil, turning the heads of all the young men by the grace of her dancing, and winning the astonished approval of the women by the cool reserve with which she received every advance of a sentimental nature. Both Mahina and Litia took jealous fancies to her—thus acquiring yet one more cause of mutual dissension—and separately poured all their woes into her ear. She was wonderfully sympathetic, and urged each one on to assert her rights and stand no nonsense; insomuch that before very long the island was fairly ringing with what Litia's people meant to do to

Mahina's, and what Mahina's would certainly do to Litia's, in the event of the King selecting one or the other.

Somebody about this time—it was never ascertained who—spread a report that Captain Saxon of the *Sybil* had a number of trade rifles on board his ship, and several cases of cartridges. The talk began to take a more dangerous turn. The schooner would not be back till the wedding was over, it was said, but let the winning party look out for themselves when she did come! The Lialians, under missionary rule, had been peaceful and law-abiding people for almost a whole generation; but they had not yet forgotten that they were once the masters of the Pacific, and that of all the warlike island races, none had been such fighters as they.... The older men began to snuff battle in the air, walked about with their chests flung out, and told bloodthirsty ancient stories to the younger Lialians. The women sang war songs at the evening gatherings in the chief-houses, and Mahina and Litia began to go about followed by bands of eager partisans. Liali was certainly warming up.

# CHAPTER XX

## QUEEN AFTER ALL

News of all these things came duly to the King through his faithful spies, and his Majesty Napoleon Timothy Te Paea III. went nearly frantic. He actually began to lose weight—a consummation that all the skill of his European court doctor had hitherto failed to bring about—and day by day he drove more wildly behind his famous blacks, covering mile after mile of lonely forest roads at a pace that brought the horses home all in a lather and the yellow satin cushions grimed with dust. The wedding approached within ten days: the triumphal arches were being erected; the Queen Consort's throne came back from the carpenter, freshly gilded and upholstered; and the band were hard at work practising the strange conglomeration of shrieks and wails that make up the Lialian National Anthem. The bride's dress, provided, according to usage, by the House of Lords, arrived at the palace in a palm-leaf basket. It was a very gorgeous affair—a long, loose robe of orange satin, embroidered in scarlet by a few of the cleverest mission-school girls—and it was of a usefully indefinite size, since the difference between the massive Mahina and the waspish little Litia was almost as great as the difference (of another kind) between their respective parties. The silver-printed invitations for the white people and the chiefs—"To be present at the wedding of His Majesty King Napoleon Timothy Te Paea III. with Princess——," came up by a whale-ship from Auckland, and so did the wedding cake, largely plaster of Paris. And still the wretched King, lashed by the scourge of his own light-hearted follies, sent pacificating presents to both girls, and put off the dire decision.

It was about this time that any wayfarer passing through the casuarina forest "might have observed" a light in Vaiti's cottage late one night. There was no one to observe, however, for the wood was supposed to be devil-haunted, and no native ever passed through it save in broad daylight. When it grew toward sunset the only Lialian who would brave its dangers so far as to rush across it in the red evening light was the King himself, who had been educated in Sydney, and did not believe in devils—much. The forest road was the shortest way home from his usual circular drive, and he frequently passed by the cottage just before sunset, driving like Jehu the son of Nimshi, and looking neither to right nor to left. He had never noticed Vaiti as he passed, for she was always within the house, looking out between the cracks of the palm-leaves, where she could see without being seen.

This evening, long after the King had passed by and the dark had come down, Vaiti sat on the floor of the hut, looking very thoughtful, as she turned out the contents of her big camphorwood box by the light of a ship's hurricane lantern. She was all alone, as usual, and smoking, also as usual. There was no sound in the solitary little house but the sighing of the wind in the casuarina trees and the steady puff of the girl's cigar. Papers, letters, packets of lace, odd bits of jewellery, silk dresses, pistols, knives, collections of rope and twine, laced underclothing, cartridges, feathers, shells, cigars, pearl-inlaid boxes, revareva plumes, and a miscellaneous collection of odds and ends garnered from all the four corners of the South Seas, strewed the floor, and the box was still half full. By-and-by she came upon what she wanted—a roll of stuff done up in waxed paper. She unfastened it, and let the contents fall out across the mats under the rays of the lantern. It was a web of pure gold tissue, bright as a summer sunrise and fine as a fairy's wing—an exquisite piece of stuff, which she had acquired from a Chinese trader in Honolulu by means none too scrupulous, and hoarded away for years.

Vaiti looked at it thoughtfully, and then opened a little tortoise-shell and silver box, and spilled its contents—a shower of photographs—into her lap. They were an exceedingly various collection—naval, military, British, French, native and half-caste—but most were men, and many were young and handsome. Perhaps the best-looking of the collection was that of a young English naval officer, signed across the corner "R. Tempest," with a Sydney address, and "Must it be good-bye?" written in tiny letters under the signature. Vaiti took the picture in her hand, and looked at it so long and earnestly that her cigar went out while she gazed. She lit another, put down the photograph, and sat smoking and thinking for quite a long time.... The world was still all before her ... and the whaling ship had said that another vessel was almost sure to touch, on her way to Sydney next week.

Once in Vaiti's many-coloured history a looking-glass had proved her undoing. It was a looking-glass that proved her salvation now, at the parting of the ways. For, as she sat thinking, a brilliant picture caught her eye—her own proud, lovely head, crowned regally with a wreath of flowers, reflected in the mirror inside the lid of the box. She smiled, stretched out her hand—letting the photograph fall unnoticed to the floor from her lap—and placed a fold of the golden tissue across her head.... Yes, it looked quite like a crown—a Queen Consort's crown ... the glass gave back a truly royal picture.

Vaiti's cheeks flushed as she looked. She could hardly turn away. But the golden fold slipped off her hair, and the queenly picture was gone.

She shut the box, and with set lips took a match, lit it, and set fire to the photograph. It burned very slowly, and the flame seemed to lick sympathetically round her own heart as it crawled about the handsome, debonair, but sensual face, lit up, and then put out, the laughing eyes, crackled through the curly hair and the white naval cap, and at last reduced the whole bright picture to a little pile of feathery black ash—dead, dead, dead!

Vaiti dropped the charred fragments from her hands, and then put her head down upon the mats and lay very still....

When morning broke through the narrow door of the hut, the rays of the rising sun fell upon the figure of a girl with a cold, expressionless face, sitting upon the threshold, hard at work with needle and thread. Upon her lap lay a pile of golden gauze.

That afternoon the King drove late in the forest. The sun was near setting, and the rays were slanting long and low among the red trunks of the gloomy casuarina trees, when the spirited blacks came galloping up to the cottage. Every day they had passed it by, a still, brown nest in the shadows, where nothing moved, but this evening, as they reached the spot, something caused them to check and shy, and the King, splendid driver as he was, had some difficulty in pulling them in. When he had succeeded, he glanced at the object that had caused their fright, and saw a vision startling enough to astonish even himself.

A stranger girl of exceeding beauty stood in the midst of the forest clearing. She was dressed in a robe of magnificent golden tissue, from which the level rays of the westering sun sparkled back in a halo of almost supernatural glory. On her head was a wreath of blood-red hibiscus flowers, and her exquisite right arm, bare except for a twisted chain of gold, held up an island kava cup of carved cocoanut shell. When she saw that the King observed her, she sank on her knees, bent her neck, and raised the cup higher in both hands above her head.

It was an invitation, and one that no Lialian could possibly have refused, for the drink brewed from the kava root, and the ceremonies connected with the brewing, tasting, and giving round, are almost a religion in those islands, and many a man, in the old wild days, has died for the insult of putting aside the proffered cup. Therefore the King descended at once, tied his horses to a tree, and advanced to take the cup from the hands of this unknown woman who understood royal etiquette so well. It was his Majesty's right to have his kava, and indeed all his food and drink, proffered in this especial attitude; but half-castes and whites were sometimes careless enough to forget the honour.

He drank the great bowlful at a draught, as a king should, and, sending the cup with a twirl to the ground, according to etiquette, cast a side glance at the beautiful cup-bearer. He hated strangers and distrusted foreigners, still....

"Will you not come in and rest, O Great Chief?" asked Vaiti in Lialian.

"Who are you?" said the King, still looking half away—but only half.

"Princess of Atiu, and daughter of the great English sea-captain Saxon," replied Vaiti, drawing herself up to her full height, and looking him straight in the eyes. The King met the look full this time, and thought that Litia's eyes, Lialian though she was, were not so bright by half. And if Mahina was fatter—as she certainly was—she never had such hair, or such a coral-red mouth. And what a magnificent dress the magnificent creature wore!

He knew at once who Vaiti was, when she mentioned her rank in Atiu, for the chocolate-coloured island kings and queens understand each other's complicated genealogies quite as clearly as do their white compeers on the other side of the world—and though Atiu was a broken, half-depopulated place, annexed to the British Crown, its chiefs were of ancient lineage and high repute. Napoleon Timothy Te Paea III. hesitated a moment—stretched out his hand—withdrew it—then stretched it out again, and graciously offered it to Vaiti, as to an equal in blood.

Vaiti, glowing with gratification, yet had the happy intuition of dropping on one knee and kissing the royal hand, European fashion. The King understood it, and swelled with pleasure, remembering how Mahina had had the impudence to chuck him under the chin when he bestowed a gracious salute upon her inferior lips, and how Litia had objected altogether to get off her horse when he was passing by, as Lialian royal customs enjoined upon all riders ... What a nuisance they had both grown to be, crying and battering at the palace gates, fighting over his gifts, getting up trouble among their relatives—trouble that he now began to fear might become so serious as to bring down the interference of the British Crown. And every Pacific monarch knew what was the inevitable next move, when that game had once begun! Good-bye to his kingship, if once the British Lion laid a claw on Lialia.

"Will you not come in and rest, Great Chief?" said the humble voice of the stranger again. And the King, still shy and distrustful, and looking at Vaiti only out of the corners of his eyes, did condescend to come in.

And the next day he rested again, and the day after that. It was astonishing how easily driving seemed to tire his Majesty at this period. And all the time the wedding preparations went forward, while Mahina and Litia, with their respective factions, grew more and more jealous of each other, and more and more enraged.

But there came a day at last, four days from the wedding, when the King declared that he would make his final choice on the evening before the marriage day, and would send a herald on that night to proclaim it through the capital.

Ruru, the royal herald, who had never before had a chance to exercise his office or wear his uniform, was extremely pleased. He got out his finery at once—a Beefeater cap and tabard of crimson silk, worn with a large silk sash, and bare legs—and began a dress rehearsal that lasted, with intervals for food and sleep, until the evening of the proclamation. At sunset he went up to the palace, received the paper that contained the message, and strutting like a turkey, came out on to the open green in front, where at least a thousand Lialians—half of them Litia's friends, and half of them Mahina's—were collected. Mahina and Litia themselves, each defiantly dressed in all the bridal finery she could muster, stood in the forefront of the crowd, exchanging looks of death and hatred. It had come to this with the two women now, that either would have cheerfully died a death of slow torture, if by so doing only she could have prevented the other from winning. That she might miss the glories of the throne was not the prominent thought in Litia's mind—only that Mahina might secure them and triumph over her; and the self-same fancy agitated the ample breast of her rival, as the two stood in the cool twilight, within sound of the breakers on the reef, waiting with choking anxiety for Ruru's words.

"People of Liali!" read the herald impressively, striking an attitude, with one bare leg advanced: "His Majesty King Napoleon Timothy Te Paea III. of Liali, being sovereign by right divine, and the Lord's Anointed, also High Chief of all the Liali Islands as descendant of the Sacred Lizard, has decided to marry, according to the custom of his forefathers, and give the land of Liali an heir to our mighty crown. The wedding will take place in the mission church to-morrow, at noon and there will be a collection afterwards for expenses! If anyone comes drunk to church, or puts nothing in the plate, he will be turned out. His Majesty hereby announces that, in order to save war and dissension among his loyal subjects, and to teach some princesses to pay him proper respect, he has decided to give the honour of his hand to Princess Vaiti, daughter of Princess Rangi of Atiu, deceased, and Captain Saxon, of the schooner *Sybil*. God save the King, and you are all to go home without making a row."

It was a fine proclamation, but assuredly the order in the last clause asked too much of Lialian humanity. No one attempted to obey it. The news was received first in a dead silence of amazement, and then by a storm of shrieks, howls, questions, a wild trampling and rushing to and fro, and, last of all, by a Homeric roar of laughter. The Lialian possesses a rough but reliable sense of humour, practical joking being his especial delight; and it suddenly dawned upon the populace of Liali that the King had played the most stupendous practical joke upon them ever known in the history of the islands. Therefore these light-hearted children of the sun, instead of raiding the palace in two separate factions, lay down and rolled upon the grass, or held helplessly on to one another, roaring with laughter. The utter disconcerting of Mahina and Litia, now that all party feeling was removed from the matter, further appealed to them as a jest of the finest sort, and witticisms that would have made a trooper blush were hurled upon the disconsolate maidens from all sides. Some few there were who frowned at the triumph of a foreigner and a stranger; but Vaiti's arts had succeeded in making her popular, and the malcontents were borne down by the roar of public amusement and assent. Vaiti herself, safely hidden in the Methodist mission house, listened to the laughter far off, and felt well pleased. She had not been very sure how matters might go, and had therefore, at a bold stroke, won the favour of the Church by approaching the missionary, and assuring him of the extreme purity of her Methodism (she was, if anything, a pure heathen) and, in confidence, of the honour awaiting her. The reverend gentleman, who had long sat on thorns by reason of the power of the Seventh Day Adventist, Christian Science, and Original Shaker missions in the islands, received her with delight, and handed her over to the care of his wife, who shortly afterwards informed him that the new light of the Church was, in her opinion, a "perfect minx"—but that she supposed it was as well, under the circumstances, to make to herself friends of the mammon of unrighteousness, as the Bible enjoined, and remain on intimate visiting terms with the palace. So Vaiti spent the fateful evening under the secure protection of the Church itself, and claimed the same creditable patronage for the day of the wedding.

What of Mahina and Litia? The disappointed princesses, when the proclamation was read out, turned and stared at each other like tigresses robbed of a meal. Neither was going to be Queen of Liali—neither was going to scratch her rival's eyes out, and root up her hair, for the crime of securing the coveted honour. The very bottom of the world had dropped out—what was to follow?

For a moment they continued to stare, each scanning the other's face under a new light—the light of common feeling. Litia remembered that she and Mahina had been brought up almost as sisters in the palace of the late Queen. Mahina recalled the time when she had almost died of measles, and Litia had nursed her through. They were both deceived, both deserted, and the friends of one could never crow offensively over the other now. The thought was mingled bitter-sweet, and the two burst out crying, and dropped into each other's arms, simultaneously vowing threats of vengeance against the treacherous interloper, which—unbacked by their war-like following of friends—they knew very well they would never be able to execute. And the crowd dispersed as the sun went down.

\*     \*     \*     \*     \*

The *Sybil* made better time than was expected, after all. Her white sails lifted against the blue, from behind the nearest island, just as the royal wedding party commenced its gorgeous procession to the church. Before the ceremony was ended, the schooner had made the harbour and Saxon was ashore. He came upon an utterly deserted town, and saw not a human being until he was halfway up to the church, outside of which he perceived an immense crowd, unable to enter. Under a tree by the wayside sat one of the English traders who had failed to get a place. He greeted Saxon uproariously, and asked him if this wasn't a proper go.

"What?" asked Saxon. "Which is he marrying?"

"Oh, crikey! he doesn't know!" roared the trader—and fell back against the tree, suffocating with laughter, and utterly declining to explain.

Saxon, cursing him for a silly fool, tramped on towards the church. The procession was coming out now, and he wanted to see the show, for though he might call the coffee-coloured Lialians niggers, he quite understood the position of King Napoleon Timothy Te Paea III., and the importance to all the islands of his choice.

He got upon a bank to see the better, fixed his long-sighted sailor eyes upon the chapel door, and saw a glittering vision emerge into the sunlight, amidst the cries and cheers of the people. That was the King, in a gorgeous uniform, with his crown on his head and a long velvet mantle sweeping behind him ... and at his left hand stepped a tall, stately, slender figure, also crowned, and dazzlingly dressed all in glittering gold.... Not Mahina, certainly; not Litia either—Who was it, then? It could never be—but it was—Vaiti!

Saxon staggered off the bank, sat down, jumped up again, and clapped his hands.

"By ——, if it isn't like her, through and through!" he cried. "By ——, I'm proud of her! Queen of Liali! Queen of Liali! But——"

He stopped, and shook his head with a knowing laugh. He was not very sober.

"But—God help the King!" he said.

THE END